The U.S.
Export-Import Bank

Westview Replica Editions

The concept of Westview Replica Editions is a response to the continuing crisis in academic and informational publishing. Library budgets for books have been severely curtailed. Ever larger portions of general library budgets are being diverted from the purchase of books and used for data banks, computers, micromedia, and other methods of information retrieval. Interlibrary loan structures further reduce the edition sizes required to satisfy the needs of the scholarly community. Economic pressures on the university presses and the few private scholarly publishing companies have severely limited the capacity of the industry to properly serve the academic and research communities. As a result, many manuscripts dealing with important subjects, often representing the highest level of scholarship, are no longer economically viable publishing projects--or, if accepted for publication, are typically subject to lead times ranging from one to three years.

Westview Replica Editions are our practical solution to the problem. We accept a manuscript in camera-ready form, typed according to our specifications, and move it immediately into the production process. As always, the selection criteria include the importance of the subject, the work's contribution to scholarship, and its insight, originality of thought, and excellence of exposition. The responsibility for editing and proofreading lies with the author or sponsoring institution. We prepare chapter headings and display pages, file for copyright, and obtain Library of Congress Cataloging in Publication Data. A detailed manual contains simple instructions for preparing the final typescript, and our editorial staff is always available to answer questions.

The end result is a book printed on acid-free paper and bound in sturdy library-quality soft covers. We manufacture these books ourselves using equipment that does not require a lengthy make-ready process and that allows us to publish first editions of 300 to 600 copies and to reprint even smaller quantities as needed. Thus, we can produce Replica Editions quickly and can keep even very specialized books in print as long as there is a demand for them.

About the Book and Authors

The U.S. Export-Import Bank: Policy Dilemmas and Choices

James J. Emery
Norman A. Graham
Richard L. Kauffman
Michael C. Oppenheimer

This book assesses the politics and programs of the U.S. Export-Import Bank and their relevance to U.S. trade policy. Focusing on the direct loan program for large credits with maturities of more than five years, the authors evaluate the broad criteria employed by the Bank in its decision-making process and the resulting allocation of Bank resources. They also examine the distribution of Bank loans and subsidies across industries and relate this to key industry characteristics such as comparative advantage and export dependence.

The problems faced by the Eximbank in recent years--high borrowing costs, intensified export credit competition, limited resources, increased risks, conflicting mandates to be competitive yet self-sustaining--have given tremendous importance to the careful articulation of policy and administration of programs. The authors find Bank policies to be broadly supportive of the U.S. trade policy goals, but also identify several areas of inconsistency and lack of definition and offer alternative means of specifying criteria to overcome these problems.

James J. Emery is a staff economist with The Futures Group, a research and consulting firm, where he is responsible for research and analysis on issues in international trade and finance. Norman A. Graham is currently a senior staff member at The Futures Group, Richard L. Kauffman is a member of the faculty of the Yale School of Organization and Management, and Michael C. Oppenheimer is international vice president of The Futures Group.

The U.S. Export-Import Bank
Policy Dilemmas and Choices

James J. Emery
Norman A. Graham
Richard L. Kauffman
Michael C. Oppenheimer

Westview Press / Boulder, Colorado

HG
3754
.U5
U16
1984

Published in 1984 in the United States of America by
    Westview Press, Inc.
    5500 Central Avenue
    Boulder, Colorado 80301
    Frederick A. Praeger, President and Publisher

Library of Congress Catalog Card Number 83-16964
ISBN 0-86531-807-7

Printed and bound in the United States of America.

10 9 8 7 6 5 4 3 2 1

Contents

Tables

Preface

In this volume, we present an analysis of the criteria employed by the Export-Import Bank of the United States (Eximbank; the Bank) in supporting exports, and of the implications of these criteria and the policies they implement for U.S. trade policy. This analysis concentrates only on the direct loan program of the Bank. While the Bank engages in short- and medium-term guarantee and insurance programs, unlike these activities, direct loans involve an actual extension of credit by the U.S. government. As these loans are usually granted on more favorable terms than those available from private, commercial sources of finance, there is a subsidy involved. The criteria the Bank employs in making decisions to support requests for financing are important for several reasons. Although the Bank has maintained it does not make a conscious choice among industries, there is a de facto choice being made that is inherent in the decision-making criteria the Bank employs. As a result of these factors, the criteria employed by the Bank in its direct loan program are more complex, and perform a much more allocative role than in the short- and medium-term programs.

A number of critics have charged that the Bank concentrates its lending in a few industries and to a handful of firms. This concentration is not the result of direct targeting to these industries, but rather of the criteria the Bank imposes that effectively select these industries. It is essential, in the context of the analysis of decisionmaking at Eximbank, to interpret "criteria" broadly in order to encompass the range of policies and guidelines that are operative. The criteria originate from the various mandates of the Bank's statute, from traditional Eximbank policies, from the current environment in world trade and export finance, and from the pursuit of broader economic policy goals.

Several factors of the international economic environment today have brought official export credits to the fore as an issue in trade policy. The stagnation in economic growth in the industrial countries and steep rises in the cost of imported oil have raised the importance of exports for the United States, as merchandise exports rose from under 5 percent of the gross national product (GNP) in 1970 to 8 percent in 1981. For particular industries, exports have become the mainstay of opportunity for expansion, or even survival. Often these are capital goods industries that have grown to rely on Eximbank financing. With access to many industrial country markets limited by a variety of mechanisms for support of domestic industry, the rapidly growing developing countries have become major export markets. For these countries, financing is often the key to a project's viability. As the United States has lost the broad-based technological lead it previously held over Europe and Japan, competition in these markets has become more sensitive to other factors such as financing. Financing terms have been used more and more as an element of competitiveness, in spite of the Organization for Economic Cooperation and Development (OECD) agreements to set limits on the terms of export credits. Negotiations in the OECD continue and form a constant backdrop to official export credit activity.

Recently, high U.S. interest rates, combined with the willingness to subsidize rates on the part of other high interest rate countries, have put pressure on the Bank to increase its rate of subsidy in order to be competitive. This trend has led to what have been the first significant losses for the Bank and a reversal in its past ability to earn a net income and return dividends to the U.S. Treasury. Caught between its long-standing policy of self-sufficiency, reinforced by the current administration's budget policy, and its statutory mandate of offering competitive terms, the Bank faces a dilemma with no easy solution.

Eximbank's direct lending criteria are assuming greater importance in the current period of high demand for official export credits and increased austerity in government spending. The combination of these two factors suggests that the Bank's selection criteria will be applied more rigorously, and will play a more important role in the selection of cases for support. With the conflicting demands on its resources, the Bank is faced with the need to apply criteria more stringently and to initiate new criteria to further narrow and define the types of cases it will support. This may mean a change in the pattern of Eximbank lending rather than a continuation of the present type of direct lending program on a reduced scale.

This work is divided into seven chapters. The first chapter examines the background to the current issues facing Eximbank. This includes a brief historical perspective on the Bank's current position, a discussion of the economic rationales for the Bank's programs, and an overview of the policymaking process at the Bank.

The second chapter analyzes the criteria used by Eximbank in its direct lending program and puts them into the context of the constraints and mandates imposed on the Bank, both by its environment and by its own institutional character.

The third chapter contains a breakdown of the pattern of Eximbank lending for the period from FY 1978 to FY 1981. The value of the subsidy element inherent in Eximbank lending is calculated, and its distribution is shown across industries. In addition, the effectiveness of the direct lending program is assessed through a comparison of several important characteristics of these industries.

The fourth chapter assesses the implications of Eximbank direct lending criteria in terms of the U.S. trade policy goal of assuring access to finance for competitive exporters. The fifth chapter examines the implications of these criteria for the trade policy goal of reducing the distortions in international trade caused by export credit subsidies. The sixth chapter reviews and compares major foreign programs for financing exports. Finally, possible alternative sets of criteria and the future impact of changing conditions on export credit policy are addressed in the seventh chapter.

Much of the research for this book was supported by a joint grant from the Department of State, the Office of the U.S. Trade Representative and the Department of Commerce, but any opinions, findings, conclusions or recommendations contained in it are those of the authors and do not necessarily reflect the views of these agencies. The authors would like to acknowledge the assistance provided by Warren Reynolds at State, the contract officer for the study, as well as the guidance provided by other members of the interagency monitoring committee.

This book would not have been possible without the generous cooperation of numerous officials in the U.S. foreign trade and economic policy community. The authors would like to thank all those who thoughtfully answered our difficult questions and made their files and records available to us. These individuals include: Lisa Barry, Edward Bruchner, George Cashman, Theodore Chapman, Robert Cornell, Richard Crafton, James Cruse, David Denoon, William Donohoe, William Draper, John M. Duff, Donald Earnshaw, William Edgar, Claude Gingrich, George Heidrich, James Kean, Phil Kennedy, Bengt Kjellgren, Margaret Kostic, William Krist, John Lange, Robert Lee, Charles Leik, Howard Lewis, Charles Lord, Alexander McCullough, George Miller, Scott Monier, Clayton Norris, Steven Piper, Alan Rapoport, Donald Rousslang, William Rudolf, Robert Scinonini, Ron Silberman, Alfred von Klemperer, David Walters, Howard Weisburg and Susan Whitsitt.

Finally, the authors would like to note the special contributions made by Anthony Geber and Seamus O'Cleireacain of The Futures Group study team, and we would like to acknowledge the superb editorial assistance provided by Cathy Johnson and Beverly Pitts, and the efforts of Marion Healy, Gail Layden and June Osborne in preparing the final manuscript for publication.

1
Introduction and Overview

THE HISTORICAL BACKGROUND

The Bank serves a multiplicity of purposes and is subject to a variety of influences. Global economic conditions affect the Bank's operations policies, as do the economic policy objectives of the current administration and overriding foreign policy interests. These factors will often pull the Bank in opposite directions, and make both policymaking at the Bank and specific decisionmaking on cases a complex process. The criteria the Bank employs thus represent a complex web of guidelines intended to meet an array of goals in a changing environment.

The Export-Import Bank of Washington was established in 1934 with the primary aim of fostering Soviet-American trade. With the extension of diplomatic recognition to the Soviet Union by President Roosevelt in 1933, a surge in demand for U.S. manufactured goods, particularly capital goods and machinery, was anticipated.[1] These types of goods required financing that was not forthcoming from commercial banks; hence the Eximbank was intended to ensure that one of the primary benefits of recognition, the opening of a huge new export market for U.S. industry, would not go unrealized.

Beyond this immediate purpose of establishing a government bank to finance Soviet trade, the creation of Eximbank was also spurred by the economic conditions of the 1930s. The breakdown of the international monetary system in 1931 created a period of instability in international finance, which was compounded by the widespread defaults on international borrowings. These factors increased the risk in international financial transactions, and reversed the trend toward internationalization of capital markets that had developed in the previous decade. International trade was suffering from worldwide depression and from a host of protectionist measures designed to preserve output and employment in the industrial countries. These efforts had at best an offsetting effect, such as the competitive devaluation of currencies. In this environment Eximbank could play a modest but important role in its ability as a government bank to absorb and judge the risks in international lending and to assume that exports were not frustrated because of a lack of financing.

To meet this need, the Second Export-Import Bank of Washington was established later in 1934, specifically to finance trade with Cuba. Its mandate was soon broadened to include all countries except the Soviet Union. As the anticipated boom in exports to the Soviet Union never

1

materialized, and the problem of Russian debts to the U.S. remained unresolved, the two Banks were merged with the general authority to support exports through financing in all markets.[2] Until 1939, the Bank concentrated primarily on exports of agricultural goods and exports of capital goods that required long financing terms.

With the outbreak of war in Europe, the Bank's lending became directed toward U.S. strategic and foreign policy interests. This meant principally the extension of loans for industrial goods to non-Axis powers in Europe, and the financing of public works and other projects in Latin America to ensure Western Hemisphere stability and support for the United States. Throughout World War II, the Bank remained a fairly small institution with a lending authority of $200 million and with a minor role in both international trade policy and U.S. foreign policy. In 1945, in response to the need for reconstruction loans to Europe, the Bank was reorganized and given a new charter under the Export-Import Bank Act of 1945.[3] This Act, as amended through 1978, constitutes the basic legislation governing the Bank. The Bank's lending authority was greatly increased and its scope of activities broadened. However, its role in postwar reconstruction was short-lived, as it was superseded by the International Bank for Reconstruction and Development and the Marshall Plan.

With the task of reconstruction removed from Eximbank, it concentrated on loans to developing countries for projects that utilized U.S. goods. A major effort was made to encourage the production of strategic minerals through extending credits for the equipment and machinery required in mining and processing. The mid-1950s saw the Bank change the focus of its activities from developing countries to all countries, as it concentrated on export promotion in general. The shift was largely in response to the increasing competitiveness of Europe and Japan, which began to erode the U.S. predominance in capital goods and manufactures as reconstruction was accomplished.[4] The new emphasis on tailoring programs to give financing support to U.S. industry in cases where it was facing strong competition intensified over the following decades as export credit became an increasingly important facet of international competition.

With the advent of serious competition for U.S. exporters of capital goods and the Bank's responsiveness to the pressure of competition, the set of factors influencing Bank programs today was basically established. While the international economic environment has changed significantly, and specific program criteria have changed, the basic character of the Bank as an institution was defined by the late 1950s. The most important reason for the creation of the Bank, the inability of the private financial system to undertake financing of certain types of exports to certain destinations, remains today as a specific policy goal of the Bank, but in an entirely different setting. The most recent orientation of the Bank, that of supporting U.S. industry where financing is a key factor in international competitiveness, is perhaps the most important rationale at the moment. These factors have been the economic arguments for Eximbank, and have served as the underpinnings of the policy debate that has centered over the Bank's role in recent years.

ECONOMIC RATIONALES FOR EXIMBANK

The ability of Eximbank programs to increase exports is the most fundamental rationale for the Bank; from this are derived the more specific rationales of assuring access to finance and providing credit support where they are factors in competitiveness. Yet this basic purpose deserves inspection on its own terms in order to clearly delineate the economic issues involved. The value of increased exports has been expressed in varying terms as the resulting increases in output and employment, an improvement in the balance of trade, or the appreciation in the value of the dollar.

In the macroeconomic context of the balance of payments, an export financed by an Eximbank loan has a delayed effect. An Eximbank loan is disbursed directly to the exporter upon shipment; hence, there is no net foreign exchange activity associated with the Eximbank financed portion of the export. The cash payment portion, normally 15 percent of the export value, results in a net demand for dollars abroad for that amount. Any amount of participation finance has the same effect as the Eximbank financed portion. The impact upon the balance of payments, or foreign exchange markets, is spread out over the term of the loan. This impact is positive as amortization payments are made, and the additional positive impact of interest payments would affect the services account. A breakdown of a $100 loan in terms of its immediate balance-of-payments effects is presented as an example in Table 1.1. As is evident from the table, the current impact of the export is offset by the financed portion. In addition, importers often arrange commercial financing for the cash payment

TABLE 1.1
Balance-of-payments effects of an Eximbank direct loan

	Debit	Credit
Current Account		
Balance on Merchandise Trade		100
Capital Account		
Long Term		
U.S. Assets		
Official Loan	42.5	
Private Loan	42.5	
Short Term		
Foreign Assets	15	

Note: It is assured here that the cash payment is made by drawing down balances held with U.S. banks. Supplying or restoring these balances would create demand for dollars.

portion, which would further delay the impact of the transaction on the balance of payments.

The effect of interest payments, while positive for any loan, is less so for an Eximbank credit because the interest rates it charges are lower than the commercial rates, if they were available, for the same products. Hence, an Eximbank credit does clearly improve the trade balance, but will have a delayed effect on the balance of payments either in the fixed exchange rate context of the official reserves transactions balance, or in the floating rate context of demand in the foreign exchange market and pressure on the exchange rate. The positive effect will occur only as the loan is repaid. Eximbank loans generate this net benefit to the balance of payments only to the extent that the exports it finances are "additional," or would not have been undertaken without Eximbank financing. The additionality of Eximbank lending depends on the degree to which it directs its resources to those transactions where financing is a critical element.

It is clear that Eximbank lending does bring about an expansion of exports, to the extent that its lending is additional, and thus helps the trade balance. However, there is no clear normative significance one can attach to the trade balance. It is one component of U.S. external economic activity and is not independent of the other components such as services, transfers, and long- and short-term capital flows. There is no economic policy rationale for achieving a balance (or surplus) in trade, per se, although there is a benefit in terms of greater employment and income resulting from increased exports.

Several perspectives from the literature on commercial policies help to further define the balance-of-payments effects of Eximbank lending. To begin with, there is no theoretical basis for a commercial policy measure to be effective under a floating exchange rate regime. Consider an export subsidy (or import duty) that affects all exports (imports) evenly. An export subsidy of this sort would create an initial expansion of exports that would, ceteris paribus, lead to an appreciation of the exchange rate until such point as equilibrium was restored--i.e., the point at which the resulting appreciation exactly offsets the effect of the subsidy.[5] This conclusion is in sharp contrast to the assertion that under fixed exchange rates commercial policy can increase income, through an increase in production of traded goods, in periods of slack domestic demand. While the actual result may deviate from that predicted by theory, because of the lag in the response of exports to exchange rate changes and other imperfections, the basic conclusion remains valid. However, the asset market theory of exchange rate determination suggests that the anticipated impact of any commercial policy would be factored into expectations of exchange rate movements, resulting in immediate exchange rate appreciation without the full trade effects.[6]

For the type of commercial policy represented by Eximbank lending, an additional refinement to the above general discussion is required. Eximbank credits are targeted and selective; they do not benefit all exports or affect competing sectors equally. Hence, any expansion in exports occasioned by Eximbank lending, leading to an appreciation in the currency, adversely affects all other exports. This results in an inter-sectoral reallocation of production and resources in favor of the industries benefiting from Eximbank. The same would, of course, be true of any selective export subsidy or subsidy equivalent.

In general, the scale of Eximbank lending is small relative to trade flows and other components of the balance of payments. Levels of economic activity abroad, interest rates, the exchange rate, and a host of variables affecting factor prices all far outweigh any impact the Bank may have on U.S. export competitiveness or on the balance of payments. The justification for the Bank rests on more specific factors concerning the importance of financing to particular types of exports.

The original rationale for Eximbank's establishment in 1934, that of providing finance for exports where none was forthcoming from private sources, survives as a more specific purpose of the Bank. This rationale is based on the existence of imperfections in the international financial markets that operate to depress exports, particularly finance-sensitive exports, from what they would otherwise be. The imperfections that affect access to finance are based on either exaggerated risk perception or an unwillingness on the part of commercial banks and other institutional lenders to absorb the risk inherent in export finance. This inability to absorb risk, whether due to misperception, the application of normal standards of financial prudence, or regulatory and statutory restrictions, is not shared by the U.S. government. A government agency such as Eximbank has a better ability to absorb concentrations of risks, greater leverage in negotiating compliance, and a longer time horizon. To the extent that these factors are all operative, there is, in a broad sense, an imperfection that can be remedied by government intervention. From a narrower perspective, the imperfections constitute only the exaggeration of risk perception and of the restrictions (prudential, regulatory, and statutory) that constrain international financial activity beyond what the dictates of a healthy, stable financial system would require. Furthermore, the risk management practices of banks and financial institutions affect the type of financing they are willing to offer, whereas Eximbank faces a different set of constraints.

The factors that constrain access to finance for exports were more prevalent in the 1930s than today. The expanded activities of major banks, many of them U.S. banks, and the development of truly international capital markets in Euro-currencies have greatly increased the liquidity, adaptability, and risk-taking abilities in sources of international finance. However, international financial markets are still prone to crises of liquidity and exaggerated risk perception by less-experienced lenders.

With increasing competition for U.S. producers of exports that require financing, it is only natural that the competition extend into the realm of financing. Goods for which financing is particularly important are those that have long lives and achieve their economic value over their life span through the production of other goods or services. These capital goods lend themselves to being financed because they generate a stream of revenues to meet debt service payments. Consequently, the sale and competitiveness of these products depend in part on the availability and terms of financing. The principal competitors of the U.S. in these finance-sensitive capital goods are the other industrial countries of Europe and Japan, and increasingly the newly industrializing countries of East Asia and Latin America. The broad category of capital goods includes industrial machinery, turnkey plant installations, transportation equipment and facilities, natural resource extraction machinery, power generation equipment, communications equipment and similar goods.

The United States held an unquestioned lead in most, if not all, of these industries in the immediate postwar period. This lead was gradually eroded as the industrial countries rebuilt after the war. The ability of the United States to preserve its technological superiority became the mainstay of U.S. export competitiveness in manufactures. European and Japanese producers were forced into competing on price and, increasingly, financing. The United States also had a generally superior financial system with much broader, deeper capital markets offering longer maturities and often lower interest rates. Eximbank served to provide finance in cases where commercial financing was constrained. The evolution of European and Japanese export credit systems was in part a reaction to this U.S. advantage.

The model on which postwar industry was developed in Europe and in a different but comparable sense in Japan entailed much more government involvement than in the United States. Specific industry policies were directed at increasing productivity, maintaining employment, stimulating technological development, and expanding into foreign markets. Certain countries actively used nationalization and subsidization to direct industrial development. Where export financing was a key aspect in industrial development, it became one aspect of overall industrial policy. In addition, foreign assistance policies were more oriented toward commercial interest than strategic interest, unlike U.S. foreign aid policy. Subsidization of credit terms became relatively common by the late 1960s, leading to a new set of problems for those countries not actively engaging in subsidization. While efforts toward the exchange of information on export credits and the reduction in credit competition through the Berne Union and the OECD have had some results, subsidization and export credit competition persist.[7]

The rationale for responding to foreign use of subsidized export credits involves elements of both equity and economic efficiency. The notion that exporters should not be disadvantaged by the actions of their competitors' governments is inherent in prevailing conceptions of commercial fairness, and is explicit in both the international trade legislation of the United States and in the agreements of the Multilateral Trade Negotiations (MTN) of the General Agreement on Tariffs and Trade. For example, Section 301 of the Trade Agreements Act of 1974 provides that a private party can request action from the U.S. government to either negotiate with a foreign government to cease an unfair trade practice or retaliate against that government in an appropriate manner.[8] The Subsidies Code of the MTN sanctions the imposition of countervailing measures where a subsidy offered by a foreign government damages the industry or economic well-being of a nation.[9] The basis in equity for reciprocal action is well established, and is reflected in the requirements for offering competitive terms in the Eximbank statute.[10]

Beyond the concept of fairness, export credit subsidies create distortions in international trade that adversely affect the pattern of production in the U.S. economy. If export sales are lost solely due to subsidized foreign financing, those industries will contract, entailing the transitional costs of resource reallocation and the ongoing cost of the transfer of resources to less productive sectors.[11] On strictly theoretical grounds of economic welfare, there may not be sufficient benefits in "matching" export credit subsidies to justify the ongoing costs of subsidization.[12] If subsidies are used only temporarily, for example until a level of market penetration has been achieved, and the transitional costs in the industry are high, perhaps reinforced by barriers to entry, then there most likely will be a net benefit to the United States of neutralizing the predatory effect of export credit subsidies. The crux of the argument rests on the magnitude of these associated costs, the strategies of foreign governments and, in a related manner, the ability of international agreements to control export credit subsidization.

Providing competitive financing terms in the presence of foreign credit subsidies is perhaps the strongest rationale at the present time for Bank policies. As the U.S. technological advantage in many of the capital goods industries typically financed by official export credits has lessened or disappeared, the importance of competitive financing for these industries has increased, placing increased demands on Eximbank.

These two rationales for the Bank, that of overcoming market imperfections in export finance and offsetting foreign subsidized finance, are the origins of many of the criteria the Bank employs in its direct loan program. A third rationale for the Bank also plays a minor role in terms of the decisionmaking process at the Bank; this is that the government often finds it useful, in the context of broader policy objectives, to encourage trade relations with specific countries. Eximbank can be an effective tool in this regard, in that loans can be extended for exports without appropriating money specifically for that purpose or without utilizing other sources of funds with more cumbersome requirements. These policy objectives may be economic, as in the encouragement of trade expansion in specific industries or areas, or political in the case of Eximbank credits as a gesture of goodwill. While the facilitation of other policy goals through export credits does not by itself constitute a thorough rationale for Eximbank, it can be important in specific cases.

Before examining the criteria the Bank adheres to in its direct loan program, it is important to briefly look at the environment in which those criteria are formulated and implemented. The policymaking process of Eximbank determines much of its institutional character and exemplifies the many influences that affect the Bank.

POLICYMAKING AT EXIMBANK

Eximbank's board of directors is responsible for approving direct credit authorizations and for setting policy at the Bank. The board is composed of the chairman, the vice chairman and three directors. All board members are appointed by the president, with the approval of Congress, and no more than three may be of the same political party. The board of Eximbank is clearly a functional part of the administration, and its policies reflect the broader economic policy positions of the current administration. The board members are the primary link to other cabinet members, and they ensure that the policies the Bank pursues are in harmony with the broader policies of the administration. Under the Reagan administration, appointments to the Eximbank board have been delayed and the changeover slow. Chairman Draper did not assume his office until July 1981. A moratorium on issuance of new preliminary commitments was in effect until that time, pending the redirection in Bank policy the Reagan administration intended to pursue. Throughout the remainder of 1981 and part of 1982, Draper was accompanied on the board only by Margaret Kahliff, who remained from the previous board. Thus, he enjoyed a great degree of autonomy in redirecting the Bank's programs.

While the board sets policy guidelines for the Bank and has final authority over approval of loans, the implementation of policy and the process of preparing financing "packages" are generally the responsibility of the staff. Here the senior staff, consisting of the senior vice president, the regional and functional vice presidents, the general counsel and treasurer, plays an important role. The senior staff acts to ensure that preliminary commitments are structured in a manner consistent with the board's policies and generally oversees the activities of the loan officers in their areas.

The loan officers themselves are the primary contact for exporters and participating commercial banks. Requests for financing commitments are initiated through them, and the details of the project are reviewed in consultation with Eximbank country economists and engineers. Eximbank normally offers a separate career path for staff members, thus strengthening the institutional identity of the Bank. This is reinforced by the senior staff who are experienced career Eximbank officials. While the policy-making process works from the board down, the decisionmaking process on individual cases works from the staff up, through the senior staff and the board.

Represented as advisory members on the board are the Department of Commerce and the Office of the U.S. Trade Representative, who have input into board decisions. The National Advisory Council (NAC) on International Financial and Monetary Policies also serves in an advisory capacity to the Bank and must review authorizations of over $30 million.

While the agencies thus represented have only advisory power over the board, it is unlikely that a case would survive a strong negative vote by NAC. In practice, NAC meetings are seldom used as a deliberative forum for discussion of Eximbank cases. Agency positions on pending cases are usually established prior to board meetings, and a consensus-building process operates to delineate the degree of support for, or objection to, each case from these areas of the government. NAC also plays a role in reviewing overall Bank policies, although here again interagency meetings or informal contacts are the primary forums for communication.

Congress oversees the Bank through the Subcommittee on International Finance of the Committee on Banking, Housing and Urban Affairs of the Senate, and through the Subcommittee on International Trade, Investment and Monetary Policy of the House Committee on Banking, Finance, and Urban Affairs. The annual hearings on the budget for Eximbank are normally an occasion for review of the Bank's activities. Congress has generally been supportive of the Bank, for example, by restoring the proposed cuts in the Bank's budget for FY 1982. In addition, oversight hearings are held from time to time on Bank activities, and export credits have been discussed in the context of trade policy before the responsible committees. The Bank's statute must also be reviewed every five years, offering a further opportunity for Congress to have input into Bank policy. Control over the budget is Congress' most immediate channel of influence.

In summary, the major outside influences on the Bank are the federal agencies concerned with international finance and trade. These include the Commerce Department, the Treasury Department, the Office of the U.S. Trade Representative (USTR), the State Department, the Federal Reserve, the Labor Department, and the Office of Management and Budget (OMB). These agencies have specific interests within the government in formulating policy in international trade and financial matters, and are often at odds over Eximbank policy. In an effort not to be pulled too far in one direction, the Bank tries to maintain its independence and its own special identity rather than falling closely under the wing of any one agency. The Bank has resisted pressure from Commerce and USTR to play a more aggressive role in export promotion, even though this would mean a larger, more expanded program. On the other hand, Eximbank has also sought to secure adequate program authority to enable it to operate at levels that satisfy its demand. The perspective of Treasury and OMB is to control the Bank's budget authority and the level of subsidy in its lending.

The positions of the various concerned agencies are an outgrowth of the complex process of policy formulation in international economics by the U.S. government, where no one agency has total authority. In this process, Eximbank is important both as a participant and a medium for various aspects of international economic policy. The criteria the Bank employs in its lending programs are also a specific expression of these policies, interpreted and implemented by the Bank as an independent institution.

NOTES

1. R. P. Browder, The Origins of Soviet American Diplomacy (Princeton: Princeton University Press, 1953), p. 191.

2. George Holliday, "History of the Export-Import Bank," in Paul Marer, ed., The Financing of East-West Trade (Bloomington, Indiana: International Development & Research Center, 1975), pp. 336-337.

3. U.S. Code, Vol. 12, Section 635.

4. Holliday, p. 348.

5. Russell S. Boyer, "Commercial Policy under Alternative Exchange Rate Regimes," Canadian Journal of Economics, Vol. 43 (1977), pp. 227-229. Wealth effects complicate the analysis for the short run, but the long-run implications remain.

6. Rudiger Dornbusch and Paul Krugman, "Flexible Exchange Rates in the Short Run," Brookings Papers on Economic Activity, 1976.

7. Those efforts at international control of export credit competition will be discussed further in Chapter 5.

8. Trade Act of 1974, U.S. Code, Vol. 19.

9. The Agreement on Interpretation and Application of Articles VI, XVI, and XXIII of the General Agreement Tariff and Trade, Part I.

10. See Chapter 2 on the statutory criteria for competitiveness.

11. This argument is made by James C. Cruse and Susan E. Whitsitt, "Eximbank in the 1980s," Appendix A, 1981. (Unpublished.)

12. Congressional Budget Office, "The Benefits and Costs of the Export-Import Bank Loan Subsidy Program" (Washington: CBO, 1981).

2
Criteria in the Direct
Loan Program

The origins of the criteria utilized by Eximbank lie in the economic rationales discussed in Chapter 1. These general strategies of assuring access to finance and countering the effect of subsidized foreign financing terms comprise the basic policy orientation of the Bank. As these strategies are pursued within the context of limited program resources and standards of financial prudence, the Bank must be selective in its credit extensions; the criteria the Bank employs determine which requests will receive support. These criteria take three basic forms: statutory requirements and restrictions, formal bank policies, and informal policies and procedures. The statutory criteria represent, of course, the influence of Congress; formal bank policies generally emanate from the board and the concerned federal agencies; informal policies and procedures originate within the Bank at both the staff and board levels.

STATUTORY REQUIREMENTS--GENERAL

The provisions of the Export-Import Bank Act of 1945, as amended to 1978, fall into two general categories. First, there are general instructions that attempt to set forth the type of policies the Bank should pursue and the role it should fill as an institution. These often require interpretation through Bank policy before becoming meaningful criteria. The second set is specific negative restrictions on Eximbank lending designed primarily to ensure the harmonization of Eximbank activity with other areas of U.S. government policy. In addition to the provisions of the Export-Import Bank Act, the budgetary limitations on the Bank's programs are included here under statutory restrictions. The general instructions are all set within the context of the stated purpose of the Bank to "aid in financing and to facilitate exports and imports and the exchange of commodities between the United States and foreign countries" (p. 1). [1]

Competitiveness

The Bank is directed to consider foreign credit competition. Specifically, the Bank is directed to charge rates and terms that are "competitive with the government-supported rates and terms and other conditions available from the principal countries whose exporters compete with U.S. exporters" (p. 4). This stipulation is reaffirmed in the 1978 Amendments to the Act (p. 22). There is further reference that the interest rate charged by its foreign counterparts should be one of the considerations in setting Eximbank rates (p. 5). In a less direct manner, there is also mention that the Bank should pay particular emphasis to the objective of "strengthening the competitive position of United States Industry" (p. 6).

Besides these stipulations on competitive rates and terms, the Bank is instructed to "seek to minimize competition in government-supported export financing" in cooperation with its foreign counterparts, and to assist other government agencies in reaching international agreement to reduce subsidized export credit (p. 4). The 1978 Amendment also included a provision for the Bank to make financing available for U.S suppliers in competition with foreign suppliers backed by subsidized credit, in excess of international agreements in a sale to a U.S. buyer (p. 23). This provision is quite specific procedurally, and calls for the Treasury to make a determination of "noncompetitive financing," to request the withdrawal of the financing, and, if no adequate response is forthcoming, to authorize Eximbank to match the foreign financing offer. This authorization is conditional on the importance of financing as a "determining factor in the sale," and the persistent offer of the foreign export credit institution. Eximbank, then, "may provide financing to match" provided the loan is otherwise in accord with statutory provisions. The Bank is not required to provide financing, but only to consider the case. To date this provision has not been fully invoked. However, as more and more goods enter the United States financed with official export credit, this provision along with the possibility of countervailing duties should act as a credible deterrent. This stipulation for loans to finance domestic sales has its origins in the case where the U.K. Export Credit Guarantee Department (ECGD) offered subsidized export credit to an American airline for the purchase of U.S. aircraft with Rolls Royce engines. The financing, which covered the full value of the airframe and engines, was reportedly a strong factor in the sale, and the reaction of the U.S. aircraft engine manufacturers led to the inclusion of this stipulation in the 1978 Amendment. This may be relatively more important for countries outside the OECD Arrangement, such as Brazil, that export capital goods to the United States, often with subsidized credit.

These various references constitute the competitiveness "mandate" in the Eximbank statute. The law leaves the determination of competitiveness of its programs up to the Bank. However, the Bank is also required to submit a semiannual report to Congress on its competitiveness, presumably to facilitate Congressional scrutiny over compliance (p. 4). The competitiveness stipulations are juxtaposed alongside other goals and restrictions that also direct the Bank's activity. For example, under the Bank's current charter, the Bank must not only offer financing at competitive terms with foreign government agencies, but also must consider the financing costs of providing competitive rates.

Believing that these two mandates were in conflict, Congress has recently acted to strengthen the Bank's competitiveness mandate. As part of the two-year rechartering bill for the Bank, the House approved language in August 1983 that would make foremost the Bank's mandate to support U.S. exports in determining interest rates; Eximbank's directors should view the average cost of money the Bank borrows from the U.S. Treasury to finance its loans as clearly secondary to providing comprehensive financing. Language drafted by the Senate Banking Committee goes even further; under the Committee's bill, the Bank would be required to be fully competitive in all its programs and to consider the cost of money in establishing interest rates only if that did not impair competitiveness (emphasis added).

Supplementary

The Bank is required to "supplement and encourage, and not compete with private capital" (p. 5). This is emphasized again with respect to agricultural exports, and the activities of the Commodity Credit Corporation (p. 11). The provision regarding supplementing but not competing with private capital is the statutory manifestation of the Bank's rationale to make up for private financial market imperfections. This, again, is a general directive and is reflected in more detail in bank policies.

Financial

There are several aspects of the statute that relate to the financial status of the Bank. The board is required to consider the Bank's cost of funds in setting interest rates on its loans, as well as its competitiveness with foreign export credit agencies (p. 4). This is the only mention in the statute of a financial guideline that suggests the Bank should be self-sufficient, and it is clearly worded to be one of two considerations. It is interesting to note that in contrast to the stipulation on interest rate charged, the Act states clearly that fees or premiums charged on guarantees and insurance "shall be charged . . . commensurate, in the judgment of the Bank, with risks covered" (p. 13). There is a stipulation that net earnings, after provision for possible losses, be paid to the Treasury as dividends, yet there is no requirement that the Bank earn a net income.

There is an overall limitation on outstanding commitments by the Bank of $40 million, against which guarantees and insurance are charged 25 percent of their face value, and loans, 100 percent (p. 18). The subtotal for guarantees and insurance is limited to $25 billion (p. 13). This overall limitation has been increased periodically in amendments to the Act, and has not served in the recent past as a resource constraint on the Bank's programs.

The Bank is also required specifically to make loans that "offer reasonable reassurance of repayment" (p. 5). The financial soundness of the project under consideration and the credit worthiness of the borrower are normal concerns of the Bank in evaluating loans. Prior to the institutionalization of competitiveness as a goal of the Bank, credit standards were the principal criteria employed. These specific criteria are discussed further under Bank procedures.

Adverse Economic Impact

The Bank is prevented from granting loans that, through the exports they support, would adversely affect other U.S. economic interests. This provision specifically refers to any loan that may affect U.S. industrial competitiveness or employment, as related to both exports of U.S. goods or imports into the United States (pp. 6, 22). Because Eximbank credits primarily finance capital goods, the intention is that the product of those capital goods not cause damage to U.S. industries in other export markets

ased imports to the United States. The 1978 Amendment
the International Trade Commission to review Eximbank's
eir domestic impact. There is specific stipulation that the
t the export of goods in short domestic supply (p. 6). This
nvoked in the period following the oil embargo of 1973 with
respec.. .. financing of oil-drilling equipment, on the basis that such
equipment was needed in the United States to expand domestic energy
production. While there is no specific statutory restriction on the
financing of energy production equipment, the Bank is instructed to make
an assessment of the impact of its loans on the availability of such
equipment in the United States (p. 4).

Small Business

The Act states that the Bank shall be mindful of the interests of
small business and of the provision of the Small Business Act (p. 5).
Eximbank has been criticized in the past for concentrating its lending to
large firms, but this is to a great extent a function of its project-related
lending criteria (see below). The universe of exporting firms is composed
of larger-sized firms than those that produce goods and services for
domestic consumption, but the Bank does lend directly to smaller firms
within that universe. Small businesses are indirect beneficiaries of
Eximbank loans through subcontracting on components of heavy machinery
and large projects. The Bank also participates in educational programs for
small businesses.

STATUTORY REQUIREMENTS--SPECIFIC NEGATIVE RESTRICTIONS

These restrictions are generally straightforward extensions of
broader U.S. policy goals. Each provision may be overridden by a
presidential determination that it is not in violation of the stated policy or
that the benefits accruing from the loan justify its extension in spite of the
conflict.

Communist Countries

Credits to Communist countries require a presidential determination,
with a separate determination necessary for each loan over $50 million
(p. 7). In addition, there are limitations as to the amount of loans that may
be authorized to the Soviet Union, with additional restrictions on loans for
energy production (p. 8). In general, Eximbank's lending policy to the
Eastern bloc countries has mirrored the stance of the United States with
regard to East-West trade, detente and overall relations with the Soviet
Union. The Bank is an important aspect of U.S. policy on East-West trade,
as capital goods from the West have been high on Eastern bloc shopping
lists. The Bank has extended to various Eastern bloc countries including
Poland, Hungary, and Romania, but to nowhere near the extent of its
European counterparts. In the current environment of U.S.-Soviet relations
and the payments' position of most Eastern European countries, further
activity in this area is unlikely. The Bank continues to lend to Yugoslavia
and the People's Republic of China.

Nuclear Nonproliferation

There is a straightforward restriction on loans to countries that violate nuclear safeguards agreements or detonate a nuclear device (except nuclear weapons states) (p. 9). The Bank is also prohibited from financing liquid metal fast breeder nuclear reactors or nuclear fuel reprocessing facilities (p. 10).

South Africa

The Bank is directed not to extend credit to the government of South Africa or to any firm in South Africa unless there is a determination that the firm does not practice apartheid (p. 12). This potential exception is detailed to such a degree as to make this provision virtually a total exclusion.

Military Goods

The Bank is prohibited from financing the sale of any military goods to less developed countries (p. 11). The Bank does not, in general, finance military sales at all. These are normally handled through facilities created expressly for that purpose, such as the Foreign Military Sales program.

Other Policy Concerns

For other considerations such as the fostering of international terrorism, environmental protection, and human rights, there must be a presidential determination made for the Bank to deny credit on "nonfinancial or noncommercial grounds" (p. 6). This provision, added in 1978, replaced an earlier stipulation that the Bank actively consider human rights as a criterion in the countries where it extends credit.[2] This change marked a turning point in the Carter human rights policy, and with the shift in the burden of proof and current administration policy, human rights no longer functions as an active criterion.

BUDGET AUTHORITY

Specific limitations on Eximbank authorizations by program are included in the Federal Budget under the Foreign Assistance Appropriations Act. Since 1978-1979 when the Bank began to emphasize competitiveness, the Bank has been actively constrained by its budget authority. It is a difficult task to judge the volume of preliminary commitments (PCs) which will be accepted and will require authorization for loans. Large projects that may be outstanding for some time, such as nuclear power plants and some telecommunications systems, pose particular problems in the allocations of the Bank's lending authority. However, the Bank carefully monitors the progress of these bid negotiations, and in a few cases is able to spread the actual authorization over several years on large projects with long disbursement schedules to even out this impact.

The budgetary restrictions on the Bank do not constitute a criterion that the Bank applies, but increase the importance of those criteria through placing a limit on available resources. There is a constant balancing act between the rates, terms and cover the Bank sets, the budget authority and the selectivity imposed by Bank policy. The Bank periodically studies the effect on loan demand of environmental factors such as international borrowing by lesser developed countries (LDCs), changes in export orders compared with changes in import orders, and the fundamental policy position of the Bank and its interest rate relative to market and competitors' rates.[3] The most important single factor in explaining changes in loan demand has been the change in Bank policy, driven primarily by the need to allocate scarce budgetary resources.[4]

There have been major criticisms of the budgetary treatment of the Bank, which will be reviewed briefly here. The first is that Eximbank does not belong in the Foreign Assistance Appropriation because it is not primarily a form of foreign aid and does not have that purpose. Groups such as the U.S. Chamber of Commerce have urged that the Bank be included in appropriation to be created for international trade, or as a separate item on its own.[5] Such a move may serve to clarify and delineate Eximbank programs within the budget but would not change its substantive treatment. A more far-reaching argument is that the budgetary authority for the Bank is more properly viewed in the light of federal credit programs because it is a program limitation and not an appropriation.[6] However, because of the concern in controlling off-budget financing and the less systematic control system for federal guarantee programs, it is unlikely that the Bank will escape inclusion in the budget.

FORMAL BANK POLICIES

This set of criteria includes explicit policies followed by the Bank. These policies are determined by the Bank itself, with input and review from NAC members and other concerned agencies. While they are expressed as explicit guidelines, they often are not absolute decisionmaking rules and entail interpretation by the board.

Interest Rate, Term and Cover

The United States supports the terms of the OECD Arrangement on Guidelines for Officially Supported Export Credit, and the Eximbank standard terms are within those specified limits. Eximbank currently charges an interest rate of 12.4 percent, 12.0 percent, or 11.0 percent, depending on the level of development of the borrower. These rates have been in effect since the most recent revisions in the Arrangement in July 1982. Prior to that time a rate of 12 percent applied to all loans, which replaced the 10.75 percent rate in November 1981.

The Bank offers direct loans in maturities of between 5 and 10 years, depending on the nature of the product and its useful life. Eximbank has selectively increased the maturity of loans beyond ten years in order to ease the annual cash payment burden and to make the loan more competitive. Amortization is made in equal semiannual installments, with a grace period during construction. This has come to be the accepted norm for official export credits, and is included in provisions of the Arrangement.

Eximbank requires a minimum cash payment of 15 percent, and does not finance local costs up to that amount as some counterparts do. Local costs are costs incurred within the importing country that are not associated directly with the importation of equipment or services. Eximbank will usually cover between 42.5 percent (one-half the financed portion) and 65 percent of the export values. A participating financial institution, normally a commercial bank or the Private Export Funding Corporation (PEFCO), will finance the remainder, often with an Eximbank guarantee (always under guarantee in the case of PEFCO). The amount of cover is varied on a case-by-case basis depending on the competitiveness of the situation. Because the final rate to the importer is a blended rate of the Eximbank portion and the financed portion, extending the cover is a means of lowering the effective rate. Eximbank also takes repayment on the later maturities, or after the participating institution has been repaid. Eximbank offers an option to increase its cover to 75 percent if the exporter agrees to finance the remaining 10 percent at a rate no higher than Eximbank's.

The Bank charges a 2 percent, one-time, front-end fee on all direct loan authorizations. This fee was instituted in July 1981 after the moratorium. Its primary purpose was to generate additional revenue to reduce the Bank's expected loss in FY 1982. Even though interest rates have been raised to more closely reflect the Bank's cost of funds, it will take time for this to affect the average (negative) spread in Eximbank's portfolio. In contrast, the front-end will have an immediate impact on current earnings.

In addition, the Bank normally complies with provisions of special sectoral agreements on aircraft and nuclear power. These call for a longer maturity for nuclear power, and a 12 percent minimum interest rate (for U.S. dollars) on aircraft. The Bank also will normally comply with the sectoral stipulations on conventional power plants and satellite ground stations. The main features of the OECD Arrangement are summarized in Table 2.1.

In the past, the Bank has adhered much less strictly to a single interest rate. Beginning in 1975, the Bank adopted a standard range of interest rates, varying with maturity, with the option of going below scale to meet foreign credit competition. With the accession to the Arrangement in 1978, the Bank generally charged rates within 100 basis points of the minimum, and on rare occasions would match other below-scale offerings, as in Tunisia in 1979. In order to emphasize predictability and offer a standard package that was within a competitive range, the Bank adopted a standard package of 65 percent cover with an 8.75 percent interest rate, plus the 10/10 supplier participation option in April 1980. Due to active export credit competition, loan demand increased and the Bank was forced to apply selective criteria to support those cases where financing was most needed for a bid to be competitive. Indeed, a surge in authorized preliminary commitments in FY 1980 exceeded the Bank's loan authority. (The Bank's planning had been disrupted because a final budget level was not clear until late in the fiscal year.) To honor these PCs the Bank entered into an extraordinary participation agreement with PEFCO to yield the rate quoted in the PC without using direct loan authority by effectively subsidizing the PEFCO rate.

The large increase in market interest rates beginning in the fall of 1979 was unmatched by a commensurate increase in Eximbank rates, so that loans with large negative spreads were continuously being added to the Bank's portfolio. The parameters of interest rate, cover, and maturity combined with the Bank's cost of fund, budget authority and the

TABLE 2.1
OECD Arrangement Guideline

	Minimum Interest Rate (%)*	Maximum Maturity (Yrs)
Country Category		
Relatively rich	12.40	5.0
Intermediate	11.35	8.5
Relatively poor	10.00	10.0
Special Sectors		
Conventional power plants		12
Ground satellite stations		8
Cash payment	15	
Amortization	Equal semiannual installments after shipment	
Sectoral "Standstills" Outside the Arrangment		
Nuclear power	None	15
Aircraft	12	10

*For medium-term credits of 2-5 years the minimum interest rates are 12.15% for rich, 10.85% for intermediate, and 10% for poor countries.

Note: This table reflects the terms agreed to as of July 1983, and does not reflect any changes resolved in subsequent negotiations.

competitive environment comprise the calculus within which the Bank attempts to balance its conflicting policies of being financially self-sustaining and competitive. In 1981, however, the prospect of losses became the overriding concern, prompting the new board to raise interest rates and institute the 2 percent commitment fee.

Financial Self-Sufficiency

While nowhere is it written down that Eximbank must earn a net income on its operations, financial self-sufficiency has been perhaps the most influential policy over the history of the Bank. In recent years this has been overshadowed by the competitiveness mandate, but is now being reaffirmed under Chairman Draper. The Bank quite consistently returned modest dividends to the Treasury until 1980, when the board decided to add all of the Bank's income to reserves. That the Bank has operated independently at a profit, has returned dividends to the Treasury, and does not actually constitute an appropriation have all been strong selling points for the Bank in Congress. Until the recent concern over export credit competition, the Bank faced fairly light scrutiny by Congress and was a popular program, in large part because of its record of self-sufficiency. The General Accounting Office does have formal responsibility for monitoring the financial conditions of the Bank, but until the past few years this financial review has been largely noncontroversial.[7]

Financial self-sufficiency exerts a strong influence over the board, as it is one measure of their effective and responsible management of the Bank. While no board wants to be associated with lack of concern for supporting U.S. exporters, neither do they want to be known as having "broken the Bank."

Foreign Content

The Bank does not finance any foreign content in projects or products. Foreign content is that portion of a project that is sourced in another country. There is no economic reason for financing exports from other countries, although some competitors, notably Great Britain and France, are much less concerned with foreign content. Foreign content financing is used as a tool of competitiveness, as it simplifies the financing for the purchaser by placing it all with one source, and subsidizes that component which may have had to be commercially financed. In large projects where there is multiple sourcing this is less of an issue because several sources of official export credit will be used, but for goods with multisource components, this can be a factor.

Adverse Economic Impact

Taking direction from its statute as noted above, the Bank will consider whether to finance an export if it can affect the competitiveness of U.S. industry. If there is any question, Policy Analysis assesses the probable impact of the export in terms of either import penetration or export competitiveness in the affected industry. This is often most problematic with product buy-back agreements, and the analysis varies depending on the type of case. In practice, while the argument may be framed in economic terms, the decision is often made on more political grounds. Adverse impact is a particularly strong criterion when the affected industry is one already undergoing adjustment to changing trade patterns, and thus more sensitive to foreign competition. The Labor Department is generally the chief spokesman for these affected industries because of the potential employment effects. In the current climate of limited resources if there is a likelihood of adverse impact, then the loan will probably not be approved. In the past the debate was often more protracted and the "double injury" argument would have carried more weight.[8]

Targeting

The criteria which together constitute the current approach of the Bank to "target" its resources span the distinction between formal and informal policies employed here. The targeting approach, formulated explicitly under Chairman Draper utilizes both a more stringent application of established criteria and the introduction of new ones. These criteria are listed in Table 2.2 and described in further detail below. The criteria are evaluated on an individual case basis, and assume varying weights in the overall decision.

Presence of Export Credit Competition

In most cases presented to the Bank for a financing commitment, there will be competition offering official financing. The Bank will often request the evidence of competition, but does not make this a requirement for consideration. Loan officers delineate the extent of foreign competition in the PC memorandum to the board. In international tender situations, the purchaser normally will give information as to who the bidders are but does not release details of competing bids prior to awards. The Exchange of Information through the OECD aids to an extent the knowledge of competitors' financing, but in many cases the Bank staff's familiarity with foreign financing systems enables them to estimate the terms of foreign offers once the competitors are known. The Exchange of Information then operates as a kind of verification.

In cases brought to the Bank as negotiated sales, with no formal competition, the Bank exerts closer scrutiny. Here the threat of competition is an implicit one, and the staff and board are forced to rely on the exporter, the importer, and their own knowledge of the industry and country for input. Clearly, the arguments of both the exporter and importer may not always be reliable, as their interest is in receiving the most favorable financing terms. While the Bank still backs cases involving negotiated sales, an exporter will have a much harder time receiving support from the Bank without documented competition.

The Bank makes a special effort to determine the use of "predatory" financing in its assessment of competition. However, information on mixed credits (the comingling of aid funds with export credits) or below-scale financing is difficult to establish. While the October 1982 negotiations produced an improved reporting procedure for mixed credits, its impact has not yet been made clear.

TABLE 2.2
Criteria employed in targeting

Existing Criteria	Newly Introduced Criteria
Export credit competition	Old generation aircraft
Monopoly position	Dependence on export markets
Rich country exclusion	Importance of financing to bid
Project/product distinction	(technological advantage and
	sensitivity of buyer to financing)

Monopoly Position[9]

The Bank applies the competition criteria in a more specific manner to U.S. producers for which there exist no competitors. Exporters with unique products are considered to be less dependent on competitive financing terms for their sales than those who face active competition. At the present time, the only products (outside of aircraft) to which this criterion is specifically applied are certain types of walking drag lines used in mining.

Aircraft

Aircraft have been the single most important industry in Eximbank direct lending, claiming between 30 percent and 50 percent of the direct loan authority each year, depending on the industry order cycle and the Bank's policy. The Bank concentrates its support on new-generation, medium-range aircraft which is the most competitive sector due to the presence of the Airbus consortium.[10]

The Bank also does not extend credit for old-generation aircraft to rich countries. The rationale is that there is no direct foreign competition for these aircraft. The Bank normally supports old-generation and long-range aircraft with financial guarantees. General aviation aircraft are occasionally financed through direct loans, but are also handled through the medium-term supplier credits programs.

Aircraft were not included in the original OECD Arrangement, although a separate "standstill" was agreed to which entailed an adherence to then current practices. However, in August 1981, in an exchange of letters, the United States and the member nations of the Airbus Industrie consortium (principally France, West Germany and the U.K) reached a "commonline" pact that set a minimum of 12 percent for dollar financings (most commercial aircraft are financed in dollars, including Airbus), maximum repayment terms of 10 years and maximum cover of 42.5 percent. Prior to the increase of Eximbank rates to the commonline in November 1981, aircraft were usually financed at a higher rate than Eximbank's standard interest rate. Eximbank's standard cover for aircraft loans is 42.5 percent, which is not increased selectively as with other product groups.

The commonline terms allow for any party at any time to call for consultation with a view to changing the agreement or to announce that it is no longer conforming to it. In addition, the pact contains a provision for review every six months. Although negotiators from the four countries have met several times since the exchange of letters to revise the accord to make it more responsive to changing market conditions, the pact has been extended several times and is now scheduled to run through July 1, 1984. For its part, the United States has expressed dissatisfaction with elements of the commonline and wishes to change a number of the commonline provisions, including a repayment term longer than ten years; self-adjusting interest rates that fluctuate in concert with commercial market rates; and freedom for Eximbank to continue to provide loan guarantees in conjunction with both floating-rate and fixed-rate sources of private financing, a provision particularly favored by the U.S. aerospace industry. Despite sustained U.S. efforts at tough repayment terms, the United States has been unsuccessful in persuading other nations, even for a time in mid-1982 threatening to unilaterally extend terms to 15 years.[11]

The current competition in medium-range aircraft is particularly intense because of the importance of follow-on sales in the aircraft industry. Airlines will be more inclined to expand their fleets by purchasing additional aircraft of the same type because of the economies inherent in standardizing maintenance, training, spares inventories, etc. In addition, subsequent purchases of spare parts significantly increase the sales generated by the initial aircraft, particularly for the engine manufacturers. Hence it is not just a one-time competition, but the establishment of a long-term market presence that will generate later sales which is at stake. The Bank's decision in July 1983 to reduce its rates to the floor of the OECD Arrangement and to increase the amount of coverage to 85 percent from 65 percent was an effort to bolster exports of such items as general aviation aircraft and helicopters.[12]

Rich Countries

Beginning in 1981, the Bank adopted several criteria to target its loans to areas, industries and cases where they can be most effective, in order to best utilize its limited resources. One aspect of this effort is the Bank's policy to avoid extending credit to rich countries. The great majority of Eximbank credits to "rich" countries, meaning the other industrial nations and the surplus oil producers, have been for aircraft. The use of export credits to finance sales to other industrial nations is an aspect of official financing the United States has been trying to reduce or eliminate, but with limited success. In terms of access to finance or buyer sensitivity to financing terms, there is little reason for Eximbank to use its resources financing exports to other industrial nations, and this is only done where competitiveness is an especially compelling argument as in recent sales of new-generation aircraft. This criterion is currently being applied much more stringently than in the past as part of the overall targeting approach.

Dependence on Export Markets

The Bank now assesses, on an industry basis, the importance of export markets to the growth of that industry and the impact of current sales on current production. In practice this has meant the identification of industries with significant order backlogs as not critically dependent on the financing terms of current sales for their long-term health and survival. The Bank formulated this criterion with the realization that some sales would be lost, but that the industry would not be hurt as badly as others competing for direct loan resources. Such a determination was made for the offshore oilfield equipment industry in 1981, and the Bank established a policy of not supporting these exports with direct credits. However, the policy was not sustained. There was a torrent of reaction from the industry claiming that it was being unfairly singled out. This pressure, combined with a drop-off in drilling activity, and hence equipment orders due to falling oil prices, led the Bank to reconsider its position and abandon that particular application of the policy. No other such determination has been made to date, and it is unclear whether the Bank will continue to identify industries on this basis as not requiring direct credit support.

INFORMAL EXIMBANK POLICIES AND PROCEDURES

This set of criteria consists of less explicit or less well-defined Bank policies and is more dependent on the decisionmaking process of the Bank staff and board. The staff is often the most influential group in terms of how these criteria operate or are applied. Many of the informal policies are the result of procedures and approaches that have been followed by the Bank for a period of years. Most involve a high degree of judgment on the part of the staff and board, who tend to be guided by established practice.

Importance of Financing to the Bid

In order to utilize its limited resources in a manner that will have the maximum effect on the Bank's support for exporters facing subsidized foreign credit competition, the Bank attempts to target its resources to those cases where financing is most important in making the sale. Case-by-case "targeting" has become an important part of the current board's policies, and although these policies are not delineated nearly enough to be explicit, formal policies, they have several identifiable components. The board believes that individual cases can be identified where the financing terms are the key element in competitiveness, and this assessment is largely made at the board level with input from the staff.

A primary basis for assessment is whether the U.S. product possesses a technological advantage over its competitors. The basic premise is that goods that are differentiated with respect to quality, technical performance, service, reputation, etc., are less sensitive to financing terms as a competitive factor in sales. With such an advantage the U.S. producer is likely to have a better chance at winning the sale on those grounds even though the financing terms are not as favorable as the competition's. A frequently cited example of this criterion is the recent sale of satellite communications equipment to Australia.[13] The board concluded that the U.S. producer, Hughes Aircraft Company, had a significant advantage in its product technology and experience. The Bank offered only a financial guarantee, and Hughes won the sale without direct credit support.

Another consideration evident in the Hughes Aircraft/Australia case was the sensitivity of the buyer to the financing terms. Australia clearly has the ability to pay market interest rates, and thus was less constrained in choosing between a superior product or lower financing costs. For many developing countries, however, resource constraints and international payments positions may result in the financing terms taking precedence over considerations of quality and performance. It is a frequently expressed opinion at Eximbank that private-sector buyers tend to be more quality conscious in their decisionmaking than state-owned corporations or government agencies. Consequently, this criterion may lead to fewer credits to private-sector buyers.

One of the problems of the case-by-case targeting approach is the difficulty of obtaining accurate information. The application of this criterion rests upon the assessment by the board and staff members involved in the case of the importance of various competitive factors. The accuracy of their assessment is dependent upon their knowledge of the exporting firm, the industry, the competition and the importer. While no doubt the board and staff are among the most qualified persons to make decisions on this basis, there is a great deal of discretion involved. In order, in part, to improve the Bank's information on select industries and the position of U.S. firms in those industries, Chairman Draper recently established the Business and International Review Division (BIRD) at the Bank. The BIRD is intended to serve as a focal point in information gathering on industries and also in tracking large cases. As with any policy designed as an initial selection procedure, monitoring the policy's success is also problematic. It is clear in cases where direct credit is denied and the export still goes ahead--as it is in cases where the export is lost even with direct credit support. The other two possible outcomes, success in the sale with direct credit support and loss with a guarantee, are ambiguous.

The importance of financing to the bid is the major determinant of the level of Eximbank support. The Bank will extend its cover to 65 percent in cases where financing is a key factor in competitiveness, and will also hold out the option of the 10-10 supplier participation agreement. The other major means of increasing the competitiveness of a bid's financing has been the extension of maturity. This was the primary tool currently used by the Bank to counter particularly concessional foreign credit terms. The extension of maturities has been the favored weapon against the "grandfathering" which has been prevalent in the period following the increase in the interest rate matrix of the Arrangement in November. While often matched by competitors, such extensions in maturity are comparatively easier for Eximbank because of the longer maturities available in the U.S. government bond market.

Project/Product Distinction

A separate criterion that the Bank has long applied is the distinction between project and product. Normally, only project financings are eligible for direct credit support, whereas products will be handled in the supplier credit programs. This determination is usually made as part of the screening process for any new request for financial support. There are several factors that influence the determination.

First, the lead time involved before the final prospect is operational is an important consideration. Generally, this means that the project must be constructed in situ as in a turnkey factory, power plant, mine, transportation facility, communication system, etc. The only major product area that does not involve a gestation period between shipment and the time it earns revenue while still enjoying direct credit support is transportation equipment. The rationale for this distinction is twofold: there is greater risk inherent in the construction phase that private sources of financing may be unwilling to assume; and the lag between shipment and revenue earning makes financing a relatively more important consideration in the viability of the project.

Second, the number of suppliers is also used to determine project status. A large number of suppliers makes the credit easier to handle, for both the Bank and the buyer, through a single loan to the buyer rather than a series of supplier credits. A large number of suppliers is also indicative of the complexity of the project.

Third, the size of the project is an implicit criterion. Formerly, the Bank had an explicit cut-off of $5 million for direct credits. Although this is no longer a stated policy, it is clearly still a rough guideline that the Bank uses. However, even as a guideline it may be increasingly irrelevant, since the cost of any project, otherwise construed, has escalated significantly in recent years. This is not to say the Bank discriminates against small exporters, but that transaction size is one factor determining direct credit eligibility. Indeed, loan officers typically expend proportionately greater time and effort on smaller transactions since they require the same procedure. Moreover, smaller exporters may not be as experienced in working with the Bank and, therefore, require greater loan officer participation in packaging a transaction.

Finally, the useful life of a project is also a consideration in the project/product determination. A long-payback period for a project is, of course, easier to finance on longer terms. The Bank tries to match the useful life of a project with the term of the loan. This is often difficult in projects with many different components, and the Bank tends to "bundle" these components together into a direct loan. For example, construction machinery may be a part of a project's financing, but its use will be limited to the early stages of the project and it may have a short product life. Also, fuel rod assemblies are often financed along with nuclear power plants, even though their useful life is roughly three years. Spare parts and credit memoranda for unspecified spares may often be as much as 15 percent of the purchase price of an aircraft, but these are used up in a short period of time.

The project/product distinction has played a major role in determining the types of industries and exports the Bank has financed through direct loans. This criterion more than any other has led to the concentration of Eximbank lending in big-ticket, long-gestation, long-payback types of industries. Large, long-term projects are more sensitive to financing terms. Therefore, these projects are quite naturally the ones for which the greatest competition in export credits has developed.

Strategic Considerations

As was mentioned with respect to fleet-building and follow-on sales in the aircraft industry, strategic considerations for U.S. industry and the exporter are a factor in the Bank's decision. The importance of penetrating new markets, in terms of countries and products, is not expressed as a formal policy and is difficult to weigh as a criterion. Establishing a market presence has been a goal for certain countries. An example is former French colonies in Africa, where it has been difficult for U.S. exporters to break new ground. These types of considerations are not primary motives for Eximbank support, but can be important as additional factors in specific cases.

Project Evaluation and Financial Analysis

Prior to the escalation in export credit competition, standards of credit worthiness were perhaps the most important criteria applied. Project viability and credit risk still are important determinants of Eximbank support, in the sense of meeting minimum standards. Eximbank engineers evaluate the technical feasibility of projects as a preliminary screening process. Utilizing a team comprised of an engineer, a loan officer, a country economist and an attorney, the viability of the project is assessed on a variety of bases.

The financial analysis undertaken by the loan officers examines the cash flow generated by the project, the sensitivity of cost and revenues to exogenous factors such as price fluctuations, and the subsequent ability of the project to service the debt. The financial condition of the buyer is also examined. This is particularly important in sales to foreign private firms.

In cases where the financial position of the firm is questionable, the Bank will request a government guarantee. The Bank is generally predisposed to lending under government guarantee rather than taking risks on the stability of private firms. The financial position and general performance of government corporations and agencies are also reviewed, although not as thoroughly.

Country risk is assessed by Bank economists. In terms of overall risk, there are certain countries "off cover" on the basis of their economic situation and international payments position. However, these are not identical to the classification of countries for short-term insurance programs. The economic climate for each specific project is also assessed. The Bank does not, as it has in the past, pay much attention to the economic suitability of the project for the country, except insofar as it affects the project's viability and cash flow projections. In riskier countries, the project is subjèct to greater scrutiny than in less risky countries. For example, in countries that the Bank views as being higher risk, a project is expected to either earn significant foreign exchange revenues or be self-liquidating in local currency. Where country risk is not substantial, the Bank may be more willing to support a financially risky project, under government guarantee.

In general, the shift in emphasis to competitiveness has resulted in a relaxation of the credit-worthiness standards of the Bank. One aspect of this relaxation is the trade-off between the two sets of criteria, and the resulting lack of consistency in standards of credit worthiness applied.

The Bank's overall exposure to individual countries is a concern in direct lending, but is not an absolute standard. The Bank does not set specific exposure limitations. Rather, it factors this concern into the overall decision, thus eliminating marginal projects that might have otherwise been supported if exposure were not a consideration.

Support for Specific Industries

As part of a broader set of U.S. government policy concerns, the Bank is committed to the support of nuclear power plant exports. As a result of the lack of new domestic orders for nuclear power stations, the industry is almost totally dependent on export markets for new orders. As most other industrial countries have their own nuclear industries, the primary markets for new orders are in the newly industrialized countries (NICs) and the less industrialized OECD members. Hence, export credits are an important aspect of government support of the industry. The coordinated support for nuclear plant exports was recently demonstrated by the State Department's denial of safeguards to the French for nuclear fuel supplies to Taiwan in the event of their winning the contracts for construction of nuclear plants there.[14] While the move was aimed at countering the French financing offer of 7-3/4 percent without lowering interest rates, it demonstrated a willingness to use leverage that has not been shown for other industries.

Export Credit Negotiations

As was mentioned above, the Bank's primary tool for increasing its competitiveness has been the extension of the maturity on direct loans. In addition to countering especially concessional credit terms, derogations on maturity have also been aimed at inducing cooperation in the reduction of subsidies in export credits through the OECD Arrangement. In the period preceding the 1982 negotiations, the Bank pursued a strategy of selective derogation on maturity aimed at influencing countries reluctant to revise the OECD Arrangement to reduce subsidies.[15]

This use of derogation on maturity for its influence beyond the outcome of the specific case is not, in practice, different from its use to increase the competitiveness of the Bank's financing. However, the motivation differs, and hence, the frequency with which this criterion is applied will vary depending on U.S. strategy in the export credit negotiations. The Bank is currently bound to adhere to the terms of the Arrangement. In the event of a lapse in the recent progress made in the OECD, or even the dissolution of the Arrangement, the extension of maturity beyond 10 years probably will become a more standard means of achieving competitiveness.

Foreign Policy Goals

Eximbank lending has been used as an instrument of foreign policy both in the withholding of export credits which is a clear statement of U.S. disapproval of a country's policies, and in extending credits as a facilitating factor where increased trade and economic relations are an important goal of U.S. foreign policy. Export credits can have an important role where imports of U.S. capital goods are desired, as in the NICs and Eastern Europe, or where the country has extremely limited access to external finance, as was the case in the recent extension of a line of credit to Jamaica. It is relatively infrequently that direct loans are initiated for political purposes (as they were in the Jamaican case). However, they often form part of an ongoing support for increased trade with certain countries.

The actual effectiveness of Eximbank loans in furthering foreign policy goals is not clear. While there is an obvious value in achieving harmony of U.S. government actions toward a country, this is most important in the negative sense. The use of Eximbank credits for foreign policy purposes has been criticized as a perversion of Eximbank resources, yet such loans have constituted a relatively small portion of authorizations in the past. In the current policy context of targeting resources, there is more limited scope for the extension of credits for political purposes, and a greater degree of usefulness must be demonstrated.

In general, there has been little coordination between U.S. foreign assistance policy within the U.S. Agency for International Development (AID) and export credit policy. The aims and activities of the two institutions differ, and the distribution of their lending is quite different across countries.[16] However, the U.S. AID mission in Egypt has launched an experimental trade financing program to match foreign subsidized credit offers, and the Trade Development Program with AID has an export financing component. Because of the perception that its competitors (particularly by France and Japan) unfairly mixed concessional aid financing with export credits, both the House and Senate Banking Committees authorized creation of new mixed financing programs in their rechartering bills. Although the full House deleted the provision, the Committee's bill provided for a $1 billion Competitive Tied Aid Fund that was intended to combat foreign governments that employ mixed credits. Under the Senate Committee bill, Eximbank would establish mixed financing in cooperation with AID or private financial institutions. Eximbank would use combinations of its credits, loans, or guarantees with concessional financing or grants offered by AID. Although the Senate Committee did not specify how the mixed credits program would be funded, it authorizes Eximbank's chairman to set up a fund and for the administrator of AID to draw on the foreign aid budget to establish a fund, as necessary.[17]

Pressure from Exporters

Exporting firms press their case at Eximbank in a number of ways. Those firms that traditionally are heavy users of the Bank maintain contacts at all levels within the Bank and make sure that their case is heard on individual loan requests. They may also lobby in Congress and with the administration, but this is less direct and may be less effective on all but the largest cases. This contact with board members and staff at the Bank is desirable in that it keeps Bank officials in touch with industry concerns. However, it also makes it easier for them to get a hearing than for smaller exporters who have had less experience with the Bank. While smaller exporters are probably not disadvantaged by lack of knowledge of Eximbank procedures, given the willingness of loan officers to help prepare their cases, they probably are disadvantaged in not knowing the importance of making their case well known at the Bank and elsewhere in the government.

The effect of such lobbying on the Bank is difficult to assess in terms of decisions on specific cases. (Virtually all interview respondents suggested there was influence at the Bank but to differing degrees.) Major exporting firms lobby extensively in Congress, with the administration, and at the Bank over the Bank's budget and policies. In addition, associations of firms are also active in speaking out on Bank policy and budget authority levels.

Institutional Character

It is difficult to accurately identify and assess the biases that are present in any institution, including Eximbank. It is perhaps fair to say that the Bank staff prefers to follow established precedents and may not be responsive to new policy initiatives from the board. There is a strong collective identification with the Bank as an institution, and a reluctance to give up its independence to the directive of other agencies. Loan officers value their ability to structure loan packages according their own judgment on what is necessary in terms of standards of credit worthiness and competitiveness. They appear to be unsympathetic to the addition of other policy constraints. The influence of the senior staff in the implementation of policy tends to further preserve the institutional biases that persist.

As a result, predispositions toward particular industries, countries, and firms exist and change slowly. The Bank probably has been too sympathetic to the aircraft industry, and perhaps to some other industries traditionally supported by the Bank. Experience, familiarity and the identification of the Bank's ability to serve the export finance needs of particular industries with the future of those industries are certainly all factors. The same factors apply to specific countries and firms. It is enough here to note their existence in general, and the fact that these considerations do influence the allocation of Eximbank lending.

ASSESSMENT

The exposition of criteria in this chapter points out two character-istics: the reliance on case-by-case assessment and the informed judgment of the board and staff; and the multiplicity of objectives, and hence criteria, which face the Bank. The criteria serve as general guidelines for decisionmaking, leaving a high degree of discretionary authority ultimately to the board. This is inevitable to a certain extent, given the conflicting constraints imposed on the Bank that require an element of flexibility in decisionmaking. This flexibility can also create inconsistency in terms of adherence to explicit, articulated policy goals.

The Bank has always relied on a case-by-case assessment, but several criteria currently applied by the Bank have increased the importance of individual board decisions. The use of selective extension of maturity to enhance the Bank's competitiveness has meant that the Bank's overall competitive posture is dependent upon the individual case assessments of the board, rather than on a set of explicit criteria. In a similar manner, targeting by the board's assessment of the importance of financing to the bid, while based on certain criteria, makes the allocation of Bank resources a function of the collective set of case-specific factors that influence each sale, rather than of an overall policy designed to promote allocative efficiency. Consequently, the success of the Bank's direct loan program in meeting competition with fewer resources rests on the board/staff judg-ment on an individual case basis. The need for a fairly rapid decision on issuance of a PC has resulted in no formal procedure being developed for comparing and ranking separate cases. There is no assurance of consis-tency across cases, as each case is assessed for what financing package is needed to make that particular sale. This has created a climate of uncertainty. An exporter has little advance idea of how his case will be treated. It also tends to increase the lobbying effort since there is more at stake in each board decision, and hence a greater potential return to a successful lobbying campaign.

The case-by-case assessment poses similar problems for the staff in their preparation of cases for board review. Loan officers are often unable to gauge the response of the board to a particular case, and hence may be put in a position of having structured a loan incorrectly in the board's view. The uncertainty that results makes their job more difficult. This is one factor contributing to the current low level of morale among Bank staff.

The high degree of discretion the board exercises on individual cases also increases the role of personal factors in decisionmaking. One example of this is that exporters and bankers "follow" board members on their overseas trips. They will try to time the presentation of credit applica-tions so that it comes soon after a board member has visited a country, because they are often more receptive having recently been there.

The Bank has traditionally relied on an individual case approach because of the number of conflicting pressures on its decision to extend credit. Some cases may be important for competitiveness, others because of the unavailability of other sources of finance, strategic industry considerations, foreign policy interests, their influence on export credit negotiations, etc. A set of more explicit criteria ranked by priority would reduce the Bank's flexibility to meet these different goals for occasional cases where they may be particularly important. The other federal agencies involved with the Bank benefit from this flexible approach because it allows them the opportunity to express their support or objection in cases that are particularly important to their interest. Indeed, a more explicit set of criteria would require sorting out the conflicting demands on the Bank, and the formulation of a strategic plan for the effective support of U.S. exports. Until such time, these criteria largely function as considerations to be weighted by the board in its decision-making process.

The importance of each criterion in the Bank's decisionmaking process is thus difficult to weigh. However, it is possible to summarize which criteria present considerations for the board to assess, and which constitute effective prerequisites or explicit exclusions for Bank support. This breakdown is shown in tabular form in Table 2.3.

The conflicting pressures on the board to provide competitive financing with limited and probably decreasing resources present the need for some form of targeting. The Bank has imposed explicit policies as part of this effort, as in aircraft and exports to rich countries, and has attempted another with respect to oil-drilling equipment. The fact that the application of the export dependence criteria in oil-drilling equipment was short-lived will probably deter the further application of this, as well as other, explicit criteria. It is uncertain whether the Bank would have persisted in its application of this criterion if industry backlogs had not fallen off. However, it is likely that the board will continue to rely primarily on its case-by-case assessment of the importance of financing as a means of targeting its resources. The major drawback to this method of targeting is that it has not produced a consistent, predictable pattern of support for U.S. exports.

TABLE 2.3
Classification of criteria

Considerations	Requirements/Exclusions
Technological advantage	Presence of competition
Sensitivity of buyer to financing	Aircraft
Adverse economic impact	Statutory negative restrictions
Rich countries	Monopoly position
Dependence on export markets	Foreign content
Support for specific industries	Project/product distinction
Influencing export credit negotiations	
Foreign policy goals	
Pressure from exporters	
Country risk	
Financial analysis	
Country exposure	

Note: General considerations are not included here.

31

NOTES

1. All quotes in this section are from the Export-Import Bank Act of 1945, U.S. Code, Vol. 12, Section 635. Page numbers refer to the pamphlet publication of the Act distributed by Eximbank.

2. The deleted clause read, "and shall also take into account . . . the observance and respect for human rights in the country to receive the exports supported by a loan or financial guarantee and the effect such exports may have on human rights in such country"; inserted by PL 95-143, October 26, 1977.

3. Eximbank, Policy Analysis Staff, "Factors Contributing to the Demand for Export-Import Bank Loan Authorization," January 30, 1980; and the "Update," November 12, 1981.

4. "Update," p. 2.

5. U.S. Chamber of Commerce, "Competitive Export Financing," statement approved November 11, 1981, p. 1.

6. Lisa Barry, "The Effect of Eximbank Programs on the Federal Budget," USTR, November 1980; also, Congressional Budget Office, "The Export-Import Bank: Implications for the Federal Budget and the Credit Market," Staff Working Paper, October 27, 1976.

7. The GAO has not, however, been a primary spokesman for the importance of the Bank's financial condition. Financial and Other Constraints Prevent Eximbank from Consistently Offering Competitive Financing for U.S. Exports. Report to the Congress, April 30, 1980; To Be Self-Sufficient or Competitive? Eximbank Needs Congressional Guidance. Report to the Congress, June 24, 1981.

8. Double injury refers to the argument that another country will supply the equipment anyway, thereby denying the U.S. the original export while still creating the increased capacity overseas.

9. This policy is the logical extension of the "technological advantage" criterion discussed under Informal Policies below. Because it is explicit and the Bank identifies specific products it will not support on this basis, it is included here as a formal policy.

10. Included in this category are the McDonnell Douglas DC-9-80 and DC-10-10, the Lockheed L1011-1000 and L1011-200, and the Boeing 757 and 767.

11. "Agreement Nears on Export Subsidies," Aviation Week and Space Technology (May 30, 1983), p. 217.

12. "Ex-Im Bank Cuts Rates," New York Times, Sec. D (July 15, 1983), p. 5.

13. Testimony of William Draper before the Subcommittee on Foreign Operations, House Committee on Appropriations, March 4, 1982.

14. "An Exim Sweetener for a Nuclear Contract," Business Week (December 28, 1981), p. 65.

15. Testimony of John Lange in Hearings on the Eximbank Budget before the Subcommittee on International Trade, Investment, and Monetary Policy of the House Committee on Banking Finance and Urban Affairs, April 28, 1981, p. 445.

16. Congressional Budget Office, "The Costs and Benefits of the Eximbank Loan Subsidy Program" (June 1981).

17. "House Approves Stronger Mandate for Exim Bank," Aviation Week and Space Technology (August 15, 1983), p. 22.

3
The Pattern of Eximbank Lending

The overall pattern of Eximbank lending is a result of the criteria described in the previous chapter. In this chapter, the distribution of Eximbank lending by sectors is examined and related to several industry characteristics. The main element used to quantify the distribution among industries is not the volume of loans, but the amount of the subsidy inherent in those loans. The subsidy magnitude is used because it reflects the impact upon the industry to a greater degree than the face value of direct loans. The limitations of the study do not permit the use of a strict cost/benefit calculus to delineate the net effects of the subsidy on the economy as a whole.

The distribution of Eximbank direct loans among industries is highly concentrated among a small group of capital goods. This is primarily a result of the Bank's support of project-related equipment and machinery with a term of five years or more. There is a much broader distribution of Eximbank support in the medium- and short-term programs. The sectoral concentration may vary extensively in each year because of the influence of large projects such as nuclear power stations, or of cyclical factors such as the introduction of a new generation of aircraft. The loans authorized in any year will often reflect the policies of previous years, because of the lag between issuance of a PC and its conversion to an authorization. The actual disbursement will come in stages up to a final "starting point" for amortization several years after the loan is authorized, creating a lag in the effect on the Bank's portfolio. The distribution of Eximbank direct loans by sector is shown in Table 3.1 for 1980-1981. These clearly show a concentration in aircraft and electric power plants, which together account for over 60 percent of total direct loans in each year.

THE SUBSIDY IN EXIMBANK DIRECT LOANS

The subsidy inherent in Eximbank direct loans is the most controversial attribute of the Bank's programs. If the Bank were to make its loans at market rates of interest, there would be much less concern over the size and nature of the Bank's programs. As suggested by the importance of competition in the discussion of lending criteria in the previous chapter, the terms of the Bank's direct lending and thus the level of subsidy are partially in response to foreign credit subsidies. The pressure of providing

TABLE 3.1
Eximbank direct loans by sector

Sector	1980 Loans Authorized ($ Thousands)	Percent	1981 Loans Authorized ($ Thousands)	Percent
Agriculture	8,923	0.22	4,133	0.08
Communications	351,037	8.68	344,597	6.83
Construction	38,294	0.95	94,389	1.87
Electric power	1,101,969	27.24	678,300	13.44
Manufacturing	242,052	5.98	453,250	8.98
Mining & refining	357,589	8.84	667,643	13.23
Transportation	1,819,104	44.97	2,695,131	53.42
Misc. credits	121,349	3.00	107,992	2.14
Misc. products	5,000	0.12	000	0.00
GRAND TOTAL	4,045,318	100.00	5,045,436	100.00

Source: Authorizations Report.

competitive finance is the primary reason for the subsidy in Eximbank direct loans. This orientation of the subsidy in Eximbank lending distinguishes it from subsidies aimed at fostering specific types of economic activity, and from export subsidies directed at improving the balance of trade; it is essentially a retaliatory measure to counter foreign subsidies. The effect of any subsidy is to increase economic activity above what it would have been without the subsidy. In the case of a retaliatory subsidy such as Eximbank lending, the effect is in principle to restore what would have been the allocation of production without the intervention of foreign subsidies.

The subsidy component is an important aspect of the Bank's direct loan program because it measures the cost associated with the program and gives an indication of the impact on domestic industry. While the Bank is the agent for the subsidy, the costs are transmitted through the credit markets to U.S. consumers because of the additional government borrowing required to fund the loan. The direct beneficiaries of the subsidy are the exporting sectors affected, and the importers receiving the loan at lower than market rates. The distribution of the subsidy between importer and exporter is not clear without making assumptions about the competitive situation and the exporter's pricing behavior. It is likely that some portion will accrue to the exporter, and Janos Horvath has suggested that in practice most of the subsidy benefits the exporter.[1] There is a benefit to the economy as a whole insofar as the Bank's lending program restores what would have been a market allocation of production with greater overall efficiency and higher productivity. In this manner, however, the Eximbank subsidy is a "second-best" solution which cannot exactly recreate the "best" world of no export credit subsidies. The difference lies in the fact that the subsidies, even if offsetting, will encourage a greater production of goods financed through official export credits and effectively expand the markets for those goods. The Bank's subsidy program aims to restore the allocation of production, but does so within a market for capital goods that is expanded through widespread subsidization of export credit. The net effect of the subsidy, to the extent it is effective, is then to increase production beyond the levels of the "best" situation while restoring the allocation among countries.

The subsidy is defined as the difference in financing costs between what the importer would have paid for a loan at market rates and an Eximbank loan. The subsidy is then a stream of periodic flows over the life of the loan which is discounted to yield a present value figure. For Eximbank direct credits, the calculation was made based on discrete semiannual payment periods according to the following formula:

$$S = \sum_{j=1}^{n} \frac{(i-r) \, P_j}{(1+i)^j}$$

where:

S = Present value of subsidy
i = Market interest rate
r = Eximbank interest rate
n = Total term of loan
m = Term of participation finance
P_j = Principal outstanding in period j
and P is amount of Eximbank loan for any period of participation finance (j = 1 to m);
otherwise equal to $\frac{(n-m)+1-j}{(n-m)}P$

The data for the calculation were taken from the Eximbank Authorizations to Date for FY 1978-1981. The market interest rate used is an average of yields on long-term straight Eurodollar bonds taken for the month in which the loan was authorized.

The assignment of a market interest rate poses problems in the subsidy calculation. Most developing countries that borrow from Eximbank would normally have access to floating rate loans in the Eurocurrency bank credit market. However, the current rate of a floating rate loan is no indication of its average cost over the life of the loan. In addition, short-term rates on which syndicated loans have been based have recently been higher than comparable fixed rates; an inverse of the normal yield curve. Due to the difficulties in comparing fixed rates with floating-rate loans, a fixed rate loan from the international bond markets was used as a comparison. This rate represents a market that is normally used by corporate and higher-grade sovereign borrowers. As such, it does not adequately reflect the market rate of a loan to riskier developing countries, and will understate the subsidy. The rate is also that prevailing at the time of authorization, not of disbursement, which is when a loan would actually be drawn down.

The disbursement schedule for loans was not known and was assumed to be six months before the first amortization payment. For large project loans, disbursement actually takes place over a period of time ending six months before the first repayment. The effective term of the loan is longer than the amortization period would suggest for these types of loans with long gestation or construction phases. This factor and the choice of interest rate will mean that the calculated subsidy is understated.[2]

The discount rate used is the market rate of interest. Loans are discounted back to the date of assumed disbursement. Therefore, the subsidy represents an estimate of the present value of the difference in financing costs between a loan at Eximbank rates and one at commercial rates, at the time of disbursement or shipment, based on market interest rates prevailing at the date of authorization. The total subsidy and the ratio of subsidy to loan amount and subsidy to export value are shown in Table 3.2. The subsidy/loan ratio is the rate of subsidy relative to the loan amount, and indicates the subsidy element of the direct loan programs. The subsidy/export value ratio is indicative of the overall price effect of the subsidy, and hence of the impact on the purchasers' decision calculus. A breakdown by product sector is given in Table 3.3. It is clear from the data that the Bank's subsidy has steadily increased since 1978, as Eximbank rates were not raised along with market rates, but kept low to preserve competitiveness.

The product category breakdowns show a large degree of variation among product classes. This is partly due to the influence of individual cases, such as the satellite broadcasting equipment sale to Cyprus in 1980 at a 6 percent rate. Power generation equipment is consistently more highly subsidized by both ratio measures. Reflecting the higher rates charged on aircraft loans, this product sector shows a lower subsidy ratio. The magnitude of the subsidy has grown relative to the exports supported and the volume of loans.

Any calculation of the subsidy element in the direct loan program is sensitive to the assumptions employed. As stated above, the calculation presented here is a conservative estimate, and understates the true subsidy. The major parameter influencing the magnitude of the subsidy calculation is the market interest rate series chosen. Differences of several percentage points among various interest rate series are common, which would change the spread over Eximbank rates to a much greater degree. The weighted average interest rate charged on Eximbank loans is

TABLE 3.2
Eximbank total subsidy, 1978-1981

	Subsidy Amount Thousands	Subsidy/Loan	Subsidy/Export Value
FY 1979	225,329	.059	.035
FY 1980	517,096	.127	.066
FY 1981	904,680	.179	.108

TABLE 3.3
Eximbank subsidy calculation, FY 1981

Product	Subsidy $Thousands	Percent of Total	Subsidy/ Loan	Subsidy/ Export Value
Construction equipment	6,703	0.7	.167	.098
Mining equipment	17,225	1.9	.143	.093
Oilfield equipment	39,955	4.4	.186	.088
Special industry machinery	117,577	13.0	.193	.135
Textile	1,375	0.3	.121	.073
Wood products	480	*	.116	.087
Paper industry	5,025	0.6	.151	.067
Petroleum refining	107	*	.158	.067
Chemical plant	4,541	0.5	.203	.108
Cement plant	4,541	0.5	.103	.108
Metal refining	1,763	0.2	.092	.030
Other special industry	97,798	10.8	.201	.144
Steel mills	39,761	4.4	.136	.118
Computers	210	*	.189	.080
Electric power	123,199	13.6	.197	.142
Boilers	14,081	1.6	.176	.139
Turbines	26,786	3.0	.167	.110
Power transmission	1,458	0.2	.347	.208
Switchgear, etc.	2,807	0.3	.151	.164
Coal/thermal	17,284	1.9	.131	.108
Hydroelectric	30,227	3.3	.293	.208
Nuclear	24,176	2.7	.200	.158
Gas turbine	3,763	0.4	.052	.029
Electric power, NEC	2,617	0.3	.103	.044
Communications equipment	46,489	5.1	.140	.112
Telecommunications	39,827	4.4	.140	.116
Other communications	6,662	0.7	.139	.085
Aircraft	467,115	51.6	.183	.102
Ships	2,834	0.3	.176	.087
Locomotives	22,980	2.5	.251	.169
Transportation facilities	1,336	0.1	.220	.094
Medical/education facil.	1,035	0.1	.201	.085
Engineering services	1,509	1.2	.138	.071
Multipurpose	16,756	1.9	.143	.069
TOTAL	904,680	100.00		

*Less than 0.1 percent.

(Continued)

TABLE 3.3 (Cont.)
Eximbank subsidy calculation, FY 1980

Product	Subsidy $Thousands	Percent of Total	Subsidy/ Loan	Subsidy/ Export Value
Construction equipment	1,239	0.2	.086	.044
Mining equipment	13,539	2.6	.130	.089
Oilfield equipment	15,995	3.1	.118	.067
Metalworking machinery	1,337	0.2	.135	.079
Machine tools	621	0.1	.136	.082
Rolling mills	716	0.1	.134	.077
Special industry machinery	38,570	7.5	.110	.077
Food processing	937	0.2	.084	.055
Textile	597	0.1	.095	.040
Paper	449	0.1	.088	.057
Petroleum refining	9,880	1.9	.095	.060
Chemicals	2,122	0.4	.175	.096
Metal refining	5,801	1.1	.122	.087
Other special industry	3,723	0.7	.094	.047
Steel mills	3,780	0.7	.161	.071
Computers	2,395	0.5	.136	.116
Electric power	135,941	26.3	.126	.082
Boilers	2,724	0.5	.106	.039
Turbines	7,158	1.4	.122	.098
Coal/thermal	14,587	2.8	.148	.064
Hydroelectric	7,607	1.4	.188	.115
Diesel generators	2,055	0.4	.158	.034
Nuclear	62,713	12.1	.116	.090
Gas turbine	7,716	1.5	.146	.102
Other electric power	31,381	6.0	.117	.063
Communications equipment	45,698	8.8	.150	.095
Telecommunications	23,320	4.5	.110	.064
Other communications	22,378	4.3	.191	.127
Aircraft	232,811	45.0	.137	.058
Ships	6,582	1.3	.140	.091
Locomotives	4,394	0.8	.101	.052
Pipelines	3,766	0.7	.223	.043
Transportation facilities	767	0.1	.111	.095
Medical equipment	581	0.1	.116	.058
Engineering services	463	0.1	.058	.034
Loan purchases/rescheduling	3,903	0.8	.080	.000
Multipurpose	5,334	1.0	.072	.044
TOTAL	517,096			

(Continued)

TABLE 3.3 (Cont.)
Eximbank subsidy calculation, FY 1979

Product	Subsidy $Thousands	Percent of Total	Subsidy/ Loan	Subsidy/ Export Value
Agricultural equipment	1,365	0.6	.047	.020
Construction equipment	867	0.4	.033	.019
Mining equipment	1,776	0.8	.050	.021
Oilfield equipment	144	0.1	.064	.027
Special industry machinery	25,203	11.2	.050	.036
Textile	111	*	.047	.020
Paper mill	664	0.3	.052	.028
Petroleum refining	18,434	8.2	.053	.040
Chemical plant	560	0.2	.037	.027
Cement plant	3,685	1.6	.036	.026
Metal refining	110	*	.053	.022
Other special industry	1,639	0.7	.044	.027
Steel mills	21,574	9.6	.082	.068
Electric power	54,995	24.4	.062	.048
Boilers	2,478	1.1	.044	.038
Turbines	69	*	.102	.046
Power transmission	3,307	1.5	.059	.026
Coal/thermal	17,256	7.6	.062	.047
Diesel generators	411	0.2	.046	.035
Nuclear	30,200	13.4	.066	.053
Gas turbine	1,274	0.6	.039	.024
Communications equipment	2,047	0.9	.048	.028
Telecommunications	607	0.3	.043	.030
Other communications	1,440	0.6	.050	.027
Vehicles (trucks)	4,249	1.9	.047	.020
Aircraft	67,814	30.1	.048	.023
Ships	436	0.2	.052	.034
Locomotives	1,509	0.6	.052	.023
Mass transit rail cars	173	0.1	.045	.019
Pipelines	1,955	0.9	.028	.021
Medical, etc., equipment	2,962	1.3	.051	.028
Rescheduling/loan purchase	2,900	1.3	.033	.000
Multipurpose	34,301	15.2	.102	.073
TOTAL	225,329			

*Less than 0.1 percent.

(Continued)

TABLE 3.3 (Cont.)
Eximbank subsidy calculation, FY 1978

Product	Subsidy		Subsidy/ Loan	Subsidy/ Export Value
	$Thousands	Percent of Total		
Construction equipment	408	0.9	.017	*
Oilfield equipment	936	2.0	.023	*
Machine tools	116	0.2	.013	*
Special industry machinery	10,393	22.1	.019	.012
Textile	210	1.4	.023	.010
Paper mill	190	0.4	.014	*
Printing	105	0.2	.026	.012
Petroleum refining	7,556	16.1	.018	.013
Chemicals	1,692	3.6	.022	.010
Cement	241	0.5	.014	.012
Metal refining	87	0.2	*	*
Other special industry	312	0.7	.030	.016
Steel mills	2,281	4.8	.040	.023
Electric power	21,968	46.7	.022	.015
Coal/thermal	613	1.3	.015	*
Nuclear	17,528	34.2	.020	.014
Gas turbine	3,658	7.8	.036	.020
Other electic power	169	1.3	.016	.014
Telecommunications	567	1.2	.015	*
Aircraft	3,179	7.0	.017	*
Locomotives	698	1.5	.019	*
Mass transit rail cars	110	0.2	.016	*
Pipelines	5,105	10.8	*	*
Medical, etc., equipment	182	0.4	.025	.015
Miscellaneous	82	0.2	*	*
Rescheduling/loan purchase	936	2.0	.020	.000
TOTAL	47,061			

*Less than 0.1 percent.

shown in Table 3.4, compared to the international bond rate used as an indicator of private market rates in the subsidy calculation. For comparative purposes, the average 6-month Eurodollar rate is also shown, along with the average rate for long-term U.S. government bonds, which is indicative of the Bank's actual funding costs.

The variation among the different interest rate series, and spreads over Eximbank rates, will produce a broad variation in the amount of subsidy. Table 3.5 shows the sensitivity of the subsidy calculation to the interest rate spread of private market rates over Eximbank rates. The example is calculated for a hypothetical $100 million export with 42.5 percent Eximbank direct loan cover and a ten-year maturity. From the calculation it is clear that an increase in the interest rate spread generates an increase in the subsidy which is slightly less than proportional, due to the higher effective discounting rate associated with larger spreads. For example, doubling the spread from 100 to 200 basis points slightly less than doubles the subsidy, from $1,848,000 to $3,581,000. The same sensitivity to interest rate differentials also characterizes the aggregate subsidy calculation of Eximbank loans for any period, as well as the subsidy on the total outstanding loan portfolio. The 2 percent commitment fee, intended to raise current income, is not included in these calculations. The fee has the effect of directly reducing the subsidy by its face value, in this case $850,000, regardless of the interest rate spread. The impact of including the fee is to reduce all the subsidy values by this amount, which is roughly equivalent to an average 50 basis point reduction in the spread.

The above analysis highlights the sensitivity of the calculation of the Bank's subsidy to the private interest rate used. The subsidy is also directly related to the terms the Bank offers on its loans. Under the current administration, the Bank has not lowered the interest rate to

TABLE 3.4
Direct loan and market interest rates (annual percentage rates)

	Eximbank Direct Loan[a]	International Bond Market[b]	6-Month Eurodollar	Long-Term U.S. Gov. Bond
FY 1981	8.76	14.06(5.30)	17.34(8.58)	13.24(4.48)
FY 1980	8.44	11.78(3.34)	13.76(5.32)	10.87(2.43)
FY 1979	8.31	9.52(1.21)	11.06(2.75)	8.98(0.67)
FY 1978	8.34	8.72(0.38)	7.74(-0.6)	8.24(-0.1)

Source: Eximbank, "Trends in the Direct Credit Program"; Appendix B; International Monetary Fund, International Financial Statistics.

[a]Weighted average.
[b]Simple average of monthly rates.

Note: Spreads over Eximbank rates are shown in parentheses.

TABLE 3.5
Subsidy calculation sensitivity analysis
(10-year direct loan for $100 million export at 42.5% cover)

Interest Rate Differential[a]	Subsidy Amount $ Thousands	Subsidy/Loan Amount Ratio	Subsidy/Export Value Ratio
(Basis Points)			
0	0	0	0
50	939	.022	.009
100	1,848	.043	.018
150	2,728	.064	.027
200	3,581	.084	.036
250	4,406	.104	.044
300	5,205	.122	.052
350	5,980	.141	.060
400	6,731	.158	.067
450	7,459	.175	.075
500	8,164	.192	.082

[a]Nominal difference between Eximbank direct lending rate and assumed private market rate.

Note: For the calculation, a 12 percent Eximbank rate was assumed, with the private market rate (also used as the discounting rate) equal to 12 percent plus the indicated spread.

increase its competitiveness (and hence subsidy), but has relied on increasing the proportion of the transaction covered by the direct loan and selectively extending maturities. These two measures each increase the subsidy amount, although less dramatically than an increase in interest rate differentials. Table 3.6 shows the effect on the level of subsidy of increasing cover from 42.5 percent to 65 percent, and of extending maturity beyond 10 years at 65 percent cover. The calculations are made for a hypothetical $100 million export transaction with a 2 percent interest rate differential. The extension of cover actually reduces the degree of subsidy relative to the loan amount, as it entails a proportionately greater increase in direct loan coverage than in the resulting subsidy. Incorporation of the 2 percent fee further dilutes the effect of increasing cover on the subsidy as the fee is charged on the loan amount. The calculations made with the 2 percent fee are shown in parentheses in Table 3.6.

As increasing the percentage of direct loan cover is normally the first option employed to make financing packages more competitive, the extension of maturity is shown calculated with 65 percent cover. At the current time the Bank is bound by the terms of the OECD Arrangement not to extend maturities beyond 10 years; this has been the preferred means of achieving greater competitiveness in the recent past, and is likely to be so in the future if the provisions of the Arrangement break down. Extending

TABLE 3.6
Subsidy calculation sensitivity analysis
(extended cover and maturity on Eximbank direct loan for $100 million
export with 2% interest rate differential)

	Subsidy Amount $ Thousands	Subsidy/Loan Amount Ratio	Subsidy/Export Value Ratio
Percent Cover			
42.50	3,581(2,731)[b]	.084(.064)[b]	.036(.027)[b]
46.75	3,844(2,909)	.082(.062)	.038(.029)
51.00	4,084(3,064)	.080(.060)	.041(.031)
55.25	4,301(3,196)	.078(.058)	.043(.032)
59.50	4,494(3,304)	.076(.056)	.045(.033)
63.75	4,658(3,383)	.073(.053)	.047(.034)
65.00	4,750(3,450)	.073(.053)	.048(.035)
Extension of Maturity[a]			
10 years	4,750	.073	.048
11 "	4,976	.077	.050
12 "	5,333	.082	.053
13 "	5,521	.085	.055
14 "	5,827	.090	.058
15 "	5,984	.092	.060
16 "	6,246	.096	.062
17 "	6,378	.098	.064
18 "	6,604	.102	.066
19 "	6,715	.103	.067
20 "	6,910	.106	.069

[a]With 65% cover.
[b]Calculations in parentheses include the 2% commitment fee.

maturity increases the subsidy by a less than proportional amount because of the effect of discounting on the subsidy flows in the later years.

From this discussion of the sensitivity of the subsidy calculation it is clear that the magnitude of the subsidy is extremely sensitive to the interest rate differential, and somewhat less so to the parameters of direct loan cover and maturity. However, the proportional distribution of the subsidy among exporting industries in the United States is largely unaffected by the magnitude of the subsidy calculation. The allocation of the subsidy to U.S. industries is an important trade policy concern in terms of whether the Bank is supporting competitive U.S. industries or protecting weaker ones.

INDUSTRIES SUPPORTED BY EXIMBANK DIRECT LOANS

The characteristics of the industries that the Bank supports give some indication of their role in U.S. export competitiveness and performance relative to other sectors. Most of the Bank's support is for goods that have formed the basis of U.S. comparative advantage. An indication of comparative advantage is given by Bela Balassa's concept of "revealed comparative advantage," a type of market share index.[3] The index is derived by dividing the share of U.S. exports of that product class in world exports of a specific product by the share of U.S. manufactured goods in world exports of manufactures. An index number value higher than 1.0 indicates a greater share in world markets than that of U.S. manufactures as a whole. Table 3.7 shows revealed comparative advantage calculated for the sectors the Bank supports. All but paper and textile machinery, metal working equipment, trucks and ships prove to be strong contributors to export performance based on market share.

The revealed comparative advantage data suggest that these industries are an important component of U.S. manufactured goods exports. Table 3.8 shows the share of the three major capital goods sectors in total U.S. exports of manufactures. As is evident from the table, capital goods have steadily accounted for approximately 60 percent of U.S. manufactured goods exports. Nonelectrical machinery and transport equipment are each a larger contributor to manufactured goods exports than any of the other major categories of manufactures. The composition of manufactured goods exports is an indicator of the source of industrial competitiveness in international markets. These data clearly reveal the importance of the capital goods sector in the overall competitiveness of U.S. industry internationally. Eximbank support for these sectors, then, means that government resources are being directed to those industries that are at the core of U.S. industrial competitiveness. If the Bank were supporting industries in which the United States did not possess any clear comparative advantage, and if these industries were not important contributors to manufactured goods exports, then there would be justifiable concern that the Bank's lending program constituted a protective subsidy propping up ailing industries.

The dependence of an industry on export markets is an indirect indicator of the importance of export markets to the level of production in the industry. Measured by the ratio of exports to total shipments, these data are presented in Table 3.9. With only a few exceptions, such as electrical equipment, the types of capital goods the Bank has supported are more reliant on export markets for their sales than the average for all manufacturing (available for 1978 only). These data suggest that the Bank is allocating its resources to industries that are both strong performers in export markets and dependent on those markets for a relatively large portion of their sales.

Technologically advanced industries have typically been among the most important sources of U.S. export strength. The technically sophisticated nature of most capital equipment suggests that the exports supported by Eximbank direct lending are among the more advanced U.S. industries. A useful measure of the degree of technological advancement in an industry is the level of expenditure on research and development. Tables 3.10 and 3.11 present data on the intensity of research and development (R&D) spending, expressed as a percentage of sales and as a

TABLE 3.7
U.S. revealed comparative advantage, 1978-1980

SITC		Product	1978	1979	1980
711		Steam boilers & aux. plant	1.01	1.41	1.54
712		Steam engines, turbines	.81	1.20	1.51
713		Internal combustion engines	2.16	2.12	1.98
714		Engines & motors, NES	2.53	2.61	2.84
	7148	Gas turbines	3.45	3.99	4.79
716		Rotating electric plant	1.57	1.39	1.47
718		Other power generating machinery	1.54	1.65	1.95
	7187	Nuclear reactors and parts	1.68	1.80	2.45
721		Agricultural machinery (exc. tractors)	1.91	1.88	1.94
722		Nonroad tractors	2.36	2.26	2.25
723		Civil engineering equipment, etc.	2.82	2.68	2.87
724		Textile, leather machinery	.61	.64	.60
725		Paper mill machinery	.95	.93	.97
726		Printing machinery	1.60	1.58	1.53
727		Food machinery	1.07	1.06	1.27
728		Other special industry machinery	1.08	1.12	1.22
	7281	Machine tools for special industries	.92	.95	1.02
	7283	Other mineral working machinery	1.07	1.05	1.17
	7284	Special industry machinery, NES	1.11	1.16	1.27
736		Metalworking machine tools	.91	.88	.90
	7361	Metal cutting machine tools	.68	.58	.49
	7362	Metal forming machine tools	.79	.82	.93
737		Metalworking machinery, NES	1.32	1.19	1.36
	7372	Rolling mills	.79	.87	1.45
741		Heating, cooling equipment	1.71	1.70	1.65
	7413	Industrial furnaces	1.21	1.05	1.23
742		Pumps	1.62	1.63	1.49
744		Mechanical handling equipment	1.73	1.72	1.76
745		Nonelectrical machinery, NES	1.46	1.51	1.47
752		Data processing equipment	3.28	3.07	2.88
764		Telecommunications equipment	1.41	1.30	1.22
	7641	Line telephone equipment	1.35	1.24	1.29
771		Electric power machinery, NES	.86	.76	.76
	7711	Transformers	.77	.69	.71
772		Switchgear	1.08	1.13	1.11
773		Electrical distributing equipment	1.18	1.00	.80
774		Electronic medical equipment	2.31	2.41	2.41
776		Transitors, valves, etc.	1.59	1.51	1.38
778		Electric machinery, NES	1.29	1.27	1.29
782		Lorries, special motor vehicles	1.08	.98	.77
791		Railway vehicles	1.56	1.30	1.31
792		Aircraft, etc.	4.97	4.23	4.06
793		Ships, boats	.16	.23	.42

Source: GATT, International Trade 1979/1980, U.N., International Trade Statistics.

TABLE 3.8
U.S. manufactures exports: sectoral shares
(by sector: percentage of total)

SITC	Sector	1979	1980	1981	1982
5	Chemicals	14.8	14.4	13.7	14.2
6	Basic manufactures	13.9	15.4	13.4	12.0
7	Machinery & equipment	60.4	58.8	62.0	62.3
71-75	Nonelectrical	28.4	29.1	30.8	31.6
76-77	Electrical	9.9	9.7	9.9	10.8
78-79	Transport	22.1	20.0	21.3	19.9
8	Miscellaneous manufactures	10.8	11.3	10.8	11.4

Source: U.S. Commerce Department, Business America, July 11, 1983.

percentage of capital expenditure. The first measure indicates the relative embodiment of technology in the goods produced in each sector, while the second measure indicates the importance of investment in new technologies in the capital expansion of the industries. By both measures, the sectors receiving the bulk of Eximbank direct credits are relatively R&D-intensive. However, these are general indications, and differences among industries within sectors, and among different products within industries, are not highlighted by these aggregate data. For example, the R&D intensity of cement plant equipment is certainly less than that of an advanced manufacturing plant utilizing automatically controlled machine tools. However, it is clear that Eximbank support, and hence subsidy, is flowing into sectors that are, on an aggregate level, more advanced technologically.

As a measure of industrial performance, productivity is also important as an indicator of advances in efficiency. The rate of increase in the productivity of U.S. manufacturing industries has slowed in the 1970s, and this has become a major concern of economic policy. For this reason, it would be counterproductive for Eximbank to systematically support and subsidize low productivity sectors. However, the data on productivity presented in Table 3.12 are inconclusive. Only electrical machinery clearly outpaces the average for all manufacturing, and the aerospace industry shows stagnant productivity.   In this case there may be significant distortions from the military and space-related industries, where output is a measurement problem. Normally, there is a positive association between technological advance, for which R&D intensity is usually a reasonable proxy, and productivity improvements.[4] From this general sectoral data, no distinct conclusions can be drawn regarding productivity levels and rates of change of the industries the Bank supports.

This analysis suggests that Eximbank is supporting sectors and industries that are important contributors to U.S. industrial and export strength. The support of industries with relatively greater export dependence also indicates that the Bank is supporting sectors in which exports are essential for continued growth. The data on revealed comparative advantage and R&D intensity show that in most cases the Bank is

TABLE 3.9
Export dependence (exports/shipments)

Product	1978	1979	1980	1981[a]
Nonelectric machinery				
Construction machinery	.283	.299	.386	.433
Mining machinery	.202	.242	.274	.287
Oil field machinery	.462	.479	.498	.490
Materials handling	.076	.054	.072	.065
Metal cutting machine tools	.136	.118	.119	.124
Metal forming machine tools	.240	.194	.214	.236
Tools, molds, precision equipment	.024	.025	.031	.042
Food processing	.450	.483	.559	.562
Textiles and apparel	.253	.311	.311	.315
Printing trades machinery	.274	.300	.314	.331
Furnaces and ovens	.245	.257	.291	.260
Turbine generator sets	.140	.159	.300	.322
Electrical and electronic equipment				
Transformers	.070	.076	.079	.083
Telecommunications equipment	.048	.050	.054	.060
Communications equipment other than telecommunications	.099	.096	.092	.092
Electronic components	.174	.182	.195	.200
Transportation equipment				
Motor vehicles	.029	.034	.041	.035
Aircraft	.431	.371	.370	.357
Aircraft - engines and parts	.186	.176	.213	.225
Shipbuilding and repairs	.024	.029	-	-
Average: all manufactures	.070			

Source: Predicasts Basebook, 1982.

[a]Provisional.

supporting strong U.S. industries. Beyond the level of aggregation presented here, however, the pattern of support for specific types of products may vary. The Bank's criterion of not supporting goods with no competition or significant technological advantage means that within the group of capital goods industries, which are described by the characteristics noted above, support is not going, in some cases, to the most advanced products. One cannot, however, strictly equate the existence of

TABLE 3.10
Research and development intensity
(R&D expenditures as a percentage of sales)

	1978[a]	1979[a]	1980[a]	1982[b]
Nonelectrical machinery	2.99	2.90	3.27	3.96
Electrical machinery	6.47	6.74	7.14	7.92
Aerospace	20.14	16.61	15.73	20.90
All manufacturing	2.11	2.12	2.31	2.88

Source: McGraw-Hill, Survey of Business Plans for R&D Expenditures, 1980, 1981, 1982.

[a]Actual.
[b]Planned.

TABLE 3.11
Research and development intensity
(R&D expenditures as a percentage of capital spending)

	1978[a]	1979[a]	1980[a]	1982[b]
Nonelectrical machinery	59.40	45.87	50.91	56.51
Electrical machinery	114.36	107.47	95.67	103.02
Aerospace	234.04	152.58	130.84	223.36
All manufacturing	40.23	37.18	36.86	45.45

Source: McGraw-Hill, Survey of Business Plans for R&D Expenditures, 1980, 1981, 1982.

[a]Actual.
[b]Planned.

TABLE 3.12
Labor productivity in capital goods sectors, index numbers (1968 = 100)

	1978	1979
Nonelectrical machinery	1.137	1.149
Electrical & electronic machinery	1.421	1.408
Aircraft & parts	.957	.942
All manufacturing	1.240	1.251

Source: Bureau of Labor Statistics, in National Science Foundation, Science Indicators, 1980.

competition with product maturity, lack of innovation, technical sophistication, etc. The competition for advanced, new generation aircraft is a case in point, as is nuclear power. With the exception of the technological advantage criterion, the Bank does not target its support on the basis of these industry characteristics, but on the basis of competition and the importance of official export credit financing to the industry and the particular case. However, the criteria the Bank does apply have led to a pattern of support that is consistent with the importance of these capital goods sectors to U.S. industrial performance.

NOTES

1.   Janos Horvath, "Are Eximbank Credits Subsidized: Towards an Empirical Analysis," in Paul Marer, ed: U.S. Financing of East-West Trade (Bloomington: Indiana University, 1975), p. 136.

2.   Subsidy calculations using 5-year Eurocurrency rates and 6-month LIBOR rates are considerably higher. See David P. Baron, "The Subsidy Provided by Eximbank Financing," Draft Paper, January 1982, forthcoming in book.

3.   "The Changing Pattern of Comparative Advantage in Manufactured Goods," Review of Economics and Statistics (May 1979), pp. 259-266.

4.   National Science Foundation, Science Indicators 1980 (Washington: Government Printing Office, 1981), pp. 120-121.

4
Providing Access to Finance: Implications for Trade Policy

Although providing access to finance for U.S. exporters has historically been the primary rationale for Eximbank, financial markets have changed significantly in recent years. In the 1930s international lending retracted drastically, and exports requiring long-term financing faced tremendous obstacles. In periods of credit contraction, tight liquidity often brought the exclusion of export financing, as banks were reluctant to take on international risks, especially on a long-term basis. However, since the 1960s a truly international financial market has developed in syndicated Eurocurrency loans and the Eurobond market. In addition, foreign bond markets have reopened and expanded in several countries, including the United States. Commercial banks greatly expanded their international lending activity, and U.S. banks have become leaders in international banking in the past decade. Medium-size regional banks have entered into international financings, gaining expertise and sophistication. However, 1982 had seen the rapid growth in international financial markets cease, and concerns over liquidity in the international banking system have mounted. This chapter assesses the impact of these developments in international finance on the role of Eximbank in assuring access to finance for U.S. exports.

SOURCES OF FINANCE

Access to finance for industrial and other projects is an issue primarily for developing countries. The wealthier industrial countries and oil exporters have well-developed domestic capital markets or enjoy a favored position in international capital markets. Developing countries have traditionally been net debtors, financing their economic growth with international borrowings. The primary source of commercial finance for developing countries has been syndicated Eurocurrency credits. Sources of concessional finance are the multilateral development banks and bilateral foreign assistance. While these concessional types of financing are sometimes used for projects similar to those financed with official export credits, they do not function as substitutes because of restricted eligibility. If concessional terms were available, a project would be financed on that basis before consideration of either official export credits or commercial sources.

51

The syndicated Eurocurrency credit market has grown rapidly in the past two decades to over $133 billion in 1981. Fueled by overseas holdings of dollars, and to a lesser extent of other currencies, liquidity was greatly increased, beginning in 1974, by the surpluses accumulated by the oil-producing states. Table 4.1 shows the volume of Eurocurrency credits since 1978. Loans are made by groups of commercial banks in syndication, in order to reduce the risk associated with any one transaction. Through syndication, very large credits can be arranged relatively easily and rapidly. The past few years have seen the development of "jumbo" credits of over $1 billion for large developing country borrowers. Syndicated loans are almost always made on a floating rate basis, with the normal reference rate being the London Inter Bank Offered Rate (LIBOR). Borrowers are charged a premium, or spread, over LIBOR, reflecting the risk associated with the credit. The spreads in the market as a whole have decreased substantially to the point where most borrowers now pay less than 1 percent over LIBOR, and many observers feel that spreads do not adequately differentiate risk.[1] Loans are made at floating rate of interest because they are funded by short-term deposits. Maturities available in the syndicated loan market are most often in the medium-term range of around five years. Longer maturities are also common for more-credit-worthy borrowers, but at increased costs. The Eurocurrency loan market is outside the jurisdiction of any national authority, and operates largely without government regulation.

Developing countries have accounted for between one-third and one-half of total borrowings in the Eurocurrency markets. The largest borrowers are the NICs of Latin America and East Asia. However, smaller, less developed countries also regularly tap the Eurocurrency markets. A small (less than $50 million), short-term syndicated credit is a typical first entry for a developing country in the international financial markets. With a record of borrowings gradually established, the terms will normally soften and available maturities will increase.

Several factors act to ensure that countries are not excluded from access to syndicated bank credits because of exaggerated risk perceptions.

TABLE 4.1
Volume of syndicated Eurocurrency loans
(publicly announced in period, in millions of dollars)

	1981	1980	1979	1978
Developing countries	45,154	35,054	47,964	37,290
Total	113,242	77,392	82,812	70,169

Source: World Financial Markets, Morgan Guaranty Trust Company of New York, March 1982.

First, international banking is very competitive, with a large number of participants. This factor is evidenced by the downward pressure on spreads. Second, credits to marginal, riskier countries have more profit potential for participating banks because of higher spreads. Low-average spreads in banks' portfolios increase the desirability of taking on higher-earning assets. Third, new entrants into the syndicated loan market are often welcomed for their "novelty" value in that they allow banks to further diversify their loan portfolios. Fourth, there is a longer-term benefit in bringing in new borrowers by managing a syndication in the establishment of a banking relationship. Lastly, and perhaps most importantly, managers of syndications are large multinational banks with extensive experience in international lending. They are sophisticated in their economic analysis and usually have good access to information. They are also knowledgeable in the various methods of reducing risk through the use of guarantees by development banks or export credit institutions and the use of private political risk insurance. While smaller regional banks that participate in syndications may be less experienced and sophisticated, it is the syndicate managers who play the critical role in putting together a credit. The participating banks act as providers of funds and do not take an active part in the negotiation and structuring of a credit.

These factors all act to foster accurate risk perception and facilitate access to finance for riskier countries in syndicated bank lending. However, other influences may distort accurate risk perception by banks in their international lending. Competition among banks in large markets, such as the NICs, gives borrowers leverage over banks, enabling them to exact more favorable terms or larger loans than the banks would otherwise be willing to grant. This aspect of international banking does not act to restrict access to finance, but does distort accurate risk perception. The recent increase in reschedulings of foreign debt has also induced heightened risk perception, particularly among regional banks that had been the major new entrants into international financing in recent years. While the major banks, with up to half or more of their assets in international loans, will remain active, the reluctance of regional banks to continue international lending will slow or halt the growth of the syndicated Eurocurrency market.[2]

Foreign and international bond markets also comprise a source of external financing for developing countries, although on a more limited basis. As Table 4.2 shows, developing countries account for only about 10 percent of foreign and international bond market activity. These borrowings are highly concentrated in a few countries, with Brazil, Mexico, Korea and Venezuela annually accounting for at least one-half of all developing country activity. Bond markets are more restrictive because of the distribution of bond purchasers to institutional and private investors, who are generally more conservative in their investments than international banks. The floating rate sector of the Eurobond market is usually the easiest place for a developing country borrower to establish a presence, as their distribution is more concentrated among banks. However, there may be little advantage in the terms of a floating rate note issue over a comparable syndicated credit.

The foreign bond market in the United States has been utilized by only a handful of developing countries including Mexico, Brazil, Venezuela, Korea, and Panama. This potentially large source of long-term, fixed-rate finance has been largely closed for all but the highest-grade international

TABLE 4.2
Volume of foreign and international bonds
(new issues in period, in millions of dollars)

	1981	1980	1979	1978
Developing countries	4,769	2,485	3,093	4,227
Total	53,040	41,920	40,990	34,279

Source: World Financial Markets, Morgan Guaranty Trust Company of New York, March 1982.

borrowers. Legal restrictions on portfolio holdings of foreign bonds by institutional investors play a role in limiting access, such as the common "blue sky" state laws in the insurance industry.[3] It is unlikely, due to the small portion of foreign bonds outstanding in the United States, that these limits constitute active constraints. Limits to access for developing countries are more likely to be in the normal standards of financial prudence maintained by institutional investors, combined with their inexperience in international lending to developing countries.

The existence of a large and efficient international capital market which has served as a source of financing for developing countries differs markedly from the international financial system in place when the Bank was founded. The financing available from this source, however, is limited in the maturities available and largely confined to floating rates. Through offering longer-term, fixed-rate loans, the Bank attempts to fill this gap in accord with its mandate to supplement but not compete with private sources of capital. By making longer-term, fixed-rate finance available, the Bank greatly facilitates the export of capital goods that are sensitive to financing terms.

MARKET IMPERFECTIONS AND GOVERNMENT
INTERVENTION IN EXPORT FINANCE

In examining the Bank's role in supplementing private finance, the concept of market imperfections needs further clarification. A strict definition of financial market imperfection would be the existence of barriers to free action, inadequate information, a small number of actors or transactions, or other factors that inhibit the efficient allocation of resources resulting from the free interplay of market forces. It was suggested above that the syndicated Eurocurrency credit market probably functions reasonably efficiently. The same may also be said of the international bond markets, under the proviso that they are funded by investors who may have a higher degree of risk aversion than in the bank credit market. Thus it is difficult to identify a structural or institutional market imperfection. The lack of longer-term or fixed-interest-rate finance is a market characteristic, not necessarily an imperfection.

Even though countries may have access to finance on a commercial basis at floating rates, these sources do not facilitate the large-scale projects that official export credits typically finance. These projects often have long gestation periods and long pay-back periods once they are on-stream. It is likely that many projects in developing countries would be uneconomic if financed over a medium-term period, or overly risky if financed at floating rates. Certainly some would go ahead on strictly commercial terms. Eximbank supplements the private finance available through the provision of financing terms that are essentially comparable to those in domestic capital markets. U.S. firms would normally finance capital expansions through the bond markets at fixed rates and maturities of ten years or more. Eximbank assumes the risk, with the proviso that it have "reasonable assurance of repayment," under the rationale of facilitating exports utilizing resources that are available to government agencies, particularly access to government bond markets.

To provide long-term, fixed-rate finance, what is required is the assumption of risk and provision of some type of long-term funding source. A direct loan from Eximbank is not necessary, and there is no inherent rationale for a subsidy, either through provision of lower-than-market interest rates or charging guarantee fees insufficient to cover costs. The rationale for a subsidy in export credit arises from the use of subsidized credits by competitors, as discussed in the previous chapter. To provide subsidized credit, either a direct loan from the Bank or an interest subsidy to commercial lenders is required. The pressures of providing competitive export finance have meant that the Bank has concentrated its direct lending on cases where subsidized financing was present, and has used financial guarantees in cases where risk was the paramount consideration. However, the structure of direct credits, in assuming the later maturities, originates from the rationale of supplementing the shorter maturities available from commercial sources. In the absence of subsidized competition in export credits, the provision of long-term, fixed-rate finance could be accomplished without direct loans. The provision of direct loans may be an important consideration in some cases, but for largely nonfinancial reasons. Some countries prefer to deal directly with the U.S. government in arranging finance for their imports from the United States. This is perhaps particularly the case in poorer countries with which the United States enjoys good economic and political relations. However, this factor influences a relatively small number of cases.

Under an Eximbank guarantee, commercial lenders must still be able to fund loans in long-term, fixed-rate markets. Banks have access to funds through the primarily short-term avenues of deposits, inter-bank borrowing and the issuance of their own securities. They have been increasingly unwilling, due to the volatility in interest rates in recent years, to incur the interest rate risk of lending at fixed rates over long periods, even with a guarantee of commercial and political risk. It is in this aspect of solving the problem of interest rate risk over long terms that an additional intermediary role has been filled by the Private Export Funding Corporation (PEFCO). PEFCO is a private corporation with stock held by banks and exporting firms. It funds its loans through issuing securities in the bond markets that carry Eximbank guarantees.[4] It thus functions as an intermediary to provide access to U.S. bond markets for countries purchasing U.S. exports. PEFCO's level of activity, however, has not been very high, as shown in Table 4.3. Net export loan commitments exceeded $500 million only in 1980, which was a special case due to the arrangement made with Eximbank to accommodate direct loan authorizations in excess of its budgetary limitations.

There are several reasons PEFCO has not assumed a more active role in export finance. The subsidized competition in export credits has put a premium on securing an Eximbank direct credit. In participation with Eximbank direct credits, the Bank assumes the later maturities of the loan, decreasing the term that must be commercially financed. On a ten-year direct loan with 42.5 percent cover, the commercial portion is only five years, or a medium-term credit. In addition, commercial banks are often active in arranging export loans with the Bank, and may be aggressive about taking the participation, for otherwise they would have little interest in the loan. Therefore, in cases when banks may be needed to finance the cash payment, local costs, and interest during construction, they will normally take the participation. PEFCO is of greatest value in financial guarantee-only cases, where the full amount of the loan must be privately funded.

Several factors may increase the utilization of PEFCO in the future. It has recently introduced a deferred pricing program that allows borrowers to delay the pricing of a loan until the actual disbursement. Previously, PEFCO had a problem with cancellation of loan commitments because borrowers were able to receive lower-cost financing at the time when funds were required. PEFCO has also instituted a loan purchase program to refinance loans made by commercial banks at fixed interest rates, and attempts are being made to increase the attractiveness of this program. The current targeting approach of the Bank suggests that there will be increased reliance on financial guarantee support, which lends itself a higher level of funding through PEFCO.

TABLE 4.3
Private Export Funding Corporation (PEFCO)
net export loan commitments: 1971-1981
(in thousands of dollars)

Year	Commitment	Year	Commitment
1981	120,310	1975	404,668
1980	1,455,470	1974	445,094
1979	438,277	1973	4,091
1978	149,441	1972	81,647
1977	253,918	1971(7 mos.)	98,660
1976	112,290		

Source: PEFCO 1981 Annual Report.

IMPLICATIONS FOR TRADE POLICY

The role of Eximbank in providing access to finance for capital goods exports has been overshadowed in recent years by the pressures of providing export finance competitive with the subsidized and more extensive programs of its counterparts. The issue for the Bank has become providing access to subsidized finance, which is a question related to export credit competition and distinct from the traditional role of the Bank in supplementing private sources of finance. Accordingly, the primary trade policy concerns about the Bank's programs are related to its role in reducing the distortions of subsidized credit (as discussed in the following chapter). However, the supplementary role of Eximbank may become relatively more important in the coming years, which will have implications for the Bank's operations and its ability to meet its other mandates.

The rapid expansion of international financial markets, outlined earlier in this chapter, has now reached a turning point. The first half of 1982 has seen a levelling off of activity in the Euromarkets, with only a slight increase in the first quarter and a decline in the second.[5] The heavy debt burden of several large borrowers has forced many banks to reconsider the wisdom of expanded lending, although most major banks have indicated a willingness to refinance credits as they fall due. The continued worldwide recession has affected the export industries of most countries, hindering their ability to service outstanding debt. At the same time, the rising value of the U.S. dollar has further exacerbated problems of debt service, as the bulk of lending to developing countries is denominated in dollars. For oil exporters, such as Mexico and Nigeria, these problems are compounded by a decline in foreign exchange earnings from their principal export industry due to the oversupply of oil on world markets. As a result of these factors the number of countries rescheduling foreign debts, and the amounts rescheduled, has soared in 1982. The inability of Mexico, one of the largest borrowers in international financial markets, to meet its debt repayments has forced a realization of the potential fragility of the international financial system, with so many countries laboring under heavy debt burdens.

In addition to the increased risk in lending to developing countries, problems of liquidity in the international financial system will also constrain further lending. The decline in oil prices, combined with production cutbacks among OPEC members, is reducing the surplus that has fueled liquidity in international financial markets over the past decade. The retraction of smaller regional banks from international lending will also remove what has been a source of expansion in syndicated lending in the past few years. The signs of tightening liquidity are already present: spreads have widened, reflecting the greater degree of risk perception and the need for higher returns to lure funds into international lending; and some inter-bank deposit lines have been cancelled, primarily to marginal banks.[6] The latter development is perhaps especially significant, as inter-bank borrowings are a primary funding avenue; and the termination of credit lines, even to marginal banks, is evidence of a move to retrenchment.

Increased risk and reduced liquidity in international lending will increase the importance of Eximbank's role in supplementing private sources of finance. Smaller, less-credit-worthy countries, as well as the NICs with large foreign debts outstanding, will be seeking additional sources of financing from abroad. As commercial sources of credit become harder to access, developing countries will be forced to rely even more on official and concessional sources to continue their economic development. Commercial banks may increasingly look to official export credit institutions for the protection of their guarantees, in order to overcome internal lending limits and reduce exposure to countries that are large borrowers or otherwise marginal credit risks. In the event of an international financial crisis, the role of official export credit institutions may be particularly important as a force of stability and as a source of continued financing. The United States has already shown its willingness to make efforts at easing the payments crisis in Mexico, and similar cases are likely to include Eximbank as one facet of such a policy initiative. While the impact, in terms of dollar volume of financing through export credit institutions, will be limited, this type of reorientation of priorities could have a significant impact on Eximbank's lending programs.

Any increase in demand for funds arising from a cutback in commercial financing would compete with Eximbank's limited resources for direct loans and financial guarantees. While greater leverage can be achieved through the use of financial guarantees, in terms of the export value of transactions (and flow of funds to the borrower), this would still mean a diversion of resources away from the Bank's current emphasis on meeting foreign credit competition. If the Bank were committed to meeting this demand, some relaxation in criteria, such as country risk standards, the project/product distinction, and the pressure of official export credit competition, may have to be relaxed. While it would clearly be a distortion of Eximbank's role to undertake what was simply disguised balance-of-payments financing, some volume of credits currently funded through Eurocurrency markets could be tied to specific imports and structured as export credits.

In fact, the Bank's involvement in Mexico has brought many of these issues to the fore. Following the Mexican government's decision in August 1982 to limit dollar outflows, some $500 to $600 million in claims were made by American firms against Eximbank's financial guarantees, with an additional $100 million or so in claims against business done in Argentina, Peru and Venezuela. In response to these claims and out of concern that the Bank would grant an additional $2 billion in guarantees to Mexico and Brazil, Sen. William Proxmire challenged the legality of the Banks' actions. In a letter to the Bank's chairman, Proxmire noted, "I do not believe that Congress intended that the Bank be a guarantor of last resort for the purpose of assisting foreign countries in meeting their balance of payments deficits." While Proxmire has sought legal opinion of the Bank's actions, he remarked that even if the guarantees are legal, they are a "sharp departure from the traditional role of the Bank." As a consequence, Proxmire asked the Bank to seek Congressional authorization for the guarantees. Arguing that the Banks' "actions seem to be deliberately designed to avoid scrutiny by the appropriations committees" of Congress, Proxmire argued that the Banks' guarantees should receive the same "lengthy and spirited debate in both Houses of Congress" that loan guarantees to Chrysler, Lockheed, and New York City received. As Proxmire put it, "Why should we make it easy for a foreign country to get a bail-out loan while U.S. companies and cities in financial distress must jump through all kinds of hoops to get similar relief?"[7]

A continued reorientation of Eximbank programs in this direction will increase the level of risk in its loan/guarantee portfolio, both in terms of large exposures to individual countries and loans to less-credit-worthy borrowers. Despite experiences with guarantees in Mexico, the Bank's record on uncollected loans to date has been quite good by most banking standards. A common measure of the risk in a bank's loan portfolio is losses on loans, sometimes expressed as a percentage of loans outstanding. However, Eximbank generally does not charge off loans, but carries delinquent loans on its books. For example, the Bank still carries loans made to China prior to 1946 and loans to Cuba before 1961, and has only charged off $8 million of loans since 1934.[8] Table 4.4 shows delinquent outstanding loans and rescheduled loans since 1978. Loans are classified delinquent as to payments of interest or principal once payments are

TABLE 4.4
Delinquent, rescheduled, and outstanding loans: 1977-1980

	1980	1979	1978	1977
Total delinquent loans* ($ thousand)	493,953.5	186,521.0	138,361.4	134,442.2
Increase in delinquent loans over previous year ($ thousand)	307,432.5	48,159.6	3,919.2	
Rescheduled loans ($ million)	86.3	26.9	54.3	
Outstanding loans ($ million)	13,765.1	11,859.0	11,550.2	
Delinquent & rescheduled loans / outstanding loans	.0421	.0180	.0167	
*Total Delinquent Loans excluding China and Cuba ($ thousand)	365,371.2	60,729.0	15,351.1	15,217.7
Delinquent & rescheduled loans / outstanding loans (excluding China and Cuba)	.033	.007	.006	

Source: Export-Import Bank of the United States Annual Report: 1978, 1979, and 1980.

60

TABLE 4.4A
Distribution of Eximbank loans and syndicated loans by country -1980
(in thousands of dollars)

Country	Eximbank Loans	Syndicated Loans
Korea, Republic of	776,700	1,942,000
Italy	376,796	6,268,000
Israel	301,375	---
Jordan	276,335	251,900
Canada	223,959	1,743,000
Mexico	196,571	5,971,000
United Kingdom	168,158	1,370,000
Venezuela	159,426	6,575,400
Spain	120,163	4,977,200
Japan	111,530	262,000
Indonesia	97,500	1,079,500
Angola	96,900	---
Argentina	81,317	2,544,000
Hong Kong	75,125	597,400
China (Taiwan)	66,660	143,500
Austria	66,400	---
Belgium	62,287	2,350,000
Yugoslavia	58,235	2,013,100
Brazil	57,393	5,548,700
Ivory Coast	51,000	565,200
France	49,120	1,745,000
Greece	48,149	1,498,600
Algeria	43,940	300,000
Denmark	43,930	1,720,000
Zaire	40,240	---
India	35,000	60,700
Poland	31,593	1,088,600
Romania	30,100	469,100
Philippines	28,180	1,270,400
Colombia	23,600	649,900
Australia	22,958	2,475,000
Thailand	21,508	844,300
Norway	18,419	685,000
Nigeria	15,835	849,800
Honduras	15,353	---
Mozambique	15,060	---
Sweden	14,862	5,457,000
Ireland	12,750	237,000
Tunisia	11,482	35,200
Morocco	10,500	450,000
Saudi Arabia	9,749	242,900

(Continued)

TABLE 4.4A (Cont.)
Distribution of Eximbank loans and syndicated loans by country -1980
(in thousands of dollars)

Country	Eximbank Loans	Syndicated Loans
Trinidad & Tobago	9,664	301,000
Egypt	9,518	243,200
Bahamas	7,750	35,000
Iceland	7,608	35,000
Cameroon	6,885	---
Peru	6,250	392,000
Costa Rica	6,181	167,500
Guinea	5,954	---
New Zealand	4,930	715,000
Dominican Republic	3,519	220,000
Cyprus	2,259	141,100
Sudan	2,252	---
Liberia	2,125	---
Sierra Leone	1,368	---
Gabon	1,360	100,000
Turkey	924	---
Nicaragua	541	---
Mauritania	73	---

Sources: Authorizations Report: Fiscal 1980 Year to Date, Export-Import Bank of the United States; Euromoney (February 1981); World Bank Annual Report 1981; World Financial Markets, Morgan Guaranty Trust Company of New York.

TABLE 4.4B
Distribution of Eximbank loans and syndicated loans by country -1981
(in thousands of dollars)

Country	Eximbank Loans	Syndicated Loans
Canada	1,170,396	8,522,300
Mexico	654,519	12,894,000
Australia	334,450	4,289,800
Nigeria	312,405	3,026,700
Korea, Republic of	276,900	3,923,900
United Kingdom	257,142	2,731,800
Israel	209,234	---
Japan	205,901	---
Brazil	141,445	6,883,600
Romania	120,743	337,000
Ivory Coast	95,340	595,000
Malta	93,014	---
Spain	91,892	5,446,400
Argentina	81,460	3,619,000
India	79,489	1,007,200
Philippines	68,068	1,434,200
China (Taiwan)	67,548	412,800
Malaysia	67,113	1,620,900
Portugal	66,695	1,966,000
Norway	60,324	1,344,600
Venezuela	59,516	6,149,300
China (Mainland)	57,105	136,000
Tunisia	56,872	82,600
France	55,710	3,975,600
Colombia	45,116	1,001,300
Zimbabwe	33,321	357,400
Yugoslavia	30,000	1,371,300
Ireland	27,000	1,200,200
Trinidad & Tobago	24,780	45,800
Morocco	22,300	922,800
Bahrein	22,026	---
Egypt	17,260	---
Belgium	16,806	399,100
Uruguay	14,850	181,000
Greece	12,000	1,286,500
Sweden	11,276	2,340,700
Peru	8,503	789,500
Lichtenstein	8,415	---
Turkey	8,000	100,000
Algeria	7,000	500,000
Jamaica	6,375	182,000

(Continued)

TABLE 4.4B (Cont.)
Distribution of Eximbank loans and syndicated loans by country - 1981
(in thousands of dollars)

Country	Eximbank Loans	Syndicated Loans
Netherland Antilles	6,070	---
Fiji Islands	5,100	---
Nauru	4,680	---
Costa Rica	4,151	---
Thailand	3,835	838,400
Cayman Islands	3,591	---
Angola	2,785	80,000
Gabon	2,699	---
Guyana	2,500	---
Tanzania	1,739	---

Sources: Authorizations Report: Fiscal 1981 Year to Date, Export-Import Bank of the United States; Euromoney (February 1982).

90 days past due. Any amount rescheduled is not classified as delinquent if payments are being made according to the revised schedule. In 1980, loans to Iran accounted for a $306 million increase in delinquencies. Expressed as a percentage of loans outstanding, delinquencies and reschedulings appear quite small, especially with the exclusion of the loans to China and Cuba.

Any deterioration in international financial conditions, with increased reschedulings and possibly defaults, will of course affect the Bank's portfolio. A greater degree of risk in the Bank's portfolio is further exacerbated by the lack of current income to add to its loan loss reserve. In this scenario, however, the Bank could increase its guarantee fees to reflect the additional risk. Presumably, the importance of the Bank's role in this respect will be limited in duration, until such a point where an improvement in global economic conditions restores stability and liquidity in international finance.

The Bank's role in assuming access to finance will be critical in maintaining the flow of exports to developing countries, and it is precisely this type of environment that led to the original establishment of Eximbank. The magnitude of the increase in loan/guarantee demand arising from more restrictive international markets, and hence of the change in focus of the Bank's programs, is not yet clear. It is likely that this pressure will increase to some degree, placing a new set of demands on the Bank's budget and its lending criteria.

NOTES

1. Euromoney (September 1980), p. 5

2. "The State of the Country Risk," Euromoney (February 1982), pp. 47-51.

3. "Foreign Bonds in the U.S.," in Frederick Fisher, The Eurodollar Bond Market (London: AMR, 1979).

4. Interest payments on PEFCO securities are directly guaranteed by Eximbank, and principal repayments are insured through a Trust Indenture arrangement.

5. Morgan Guaranty Trust Company, World Financial Markets (August 1982).

6. Euromoney (October 1982).

7. "Claims on U.S. Export-Import Bank to Reach $700 Million," Associated Press Wire, March 18, 1983, AM cycle; W. Dale Nelson, "Proxmire: Loan Guarantees to Mexico, Brazil, Need Congressional O.K.," Associated Press Wire, August 25, 1983, AM cycle.

8. General Accounting Office, To Be Self-Sufficient or Competitive? Eximbank Needs Congressional Guidance, Report to the Congress, June 24, 1981, p. 14.

5
Reducing the Distortions
of Subsidized Credit: Implications
for Trade Policy

Competition in export credits, spurred on by countries actively using subsidized finance as a promotion weapon, has expanded the scope of official export credit activity well beyond what is needed to compensate for a lack of access to commercial finance. In addition to export credits and guarantees, more aggressive exporting countries have developed programs for insurance against inflation and foreign exchange risk. Competition has kept interest rates on export credits well below market levels, and as a result the level of subsidization in export credits has risen dramatically, reaching roughly $5.5 billion in 1980 alone.[1] U.S. policy aimed at reducing the distortions of subsidized competition in export credits has been to seek an effective international agreement controlling export credit subsidies. These efforts have been only partially successful, and pressure has continued on Eximbank to provide export finance on competitive terms.   The Bank's direct lending program has become increasingly oriented toward competitiveness within the constraints of its budgetary authority and policy against incurring losses.

The "best" solution of elimination of credit subsidies through international negotiation and agreement is the subject of the first section of this chapter. The "second-best" response by Eximbank, and the issues posed by providing competitive finance, is the subject of the second part of the chapter. This less-than-optimum response is necessitated by the uncertain status of international agreements on export credits, which directly affects the orientation of Eximbank policy by determining the competitive environment to which the Bank must respond. The chapter concludes with an analysis of the implications of the resulting Eximbank policies for broader trade policy objectives.

INTERNATIONAL CONTROL OF EXPORT CREDITS:
THE OECD ARRANGEMENT

International agreements limiting government intervention in international trade are by their nature a result of compromise among differing national interests and trade policy goals. Compromise is necessary to ensure the inclusion of the interested or affected parties, as nations will agree to restrict their freedom of action only to the extent that their competitors accept equivalent restrictions. The omission or exclusion of key nations from international trade agreements can only increase the effectiveness of their use of trade distorting measures. As simple international trade theory suggests, all trading partners will be better-off and the volume of trade maximized if all nations refrain from distortive measures. A single nation can increase its production and income through imposition of an appropriate tariff or export subsidy if there are no retaliatory measures by others. In the presence of retaliation, the original gain by the initiating country will not be achieved, and the retaliatory measure may result in either the inclusion of outsiders in the agreement or a mutually destructive escalation of retaliation into "trade wars," or some combination of both. International agreements on trade issues are the result of these conflicting forces, and are usually fluid, constantly changing institutions built on a precarious consensus.

Negotiations toward an international agreement on control of official export credits have been ongoing in the OECD since 1963. However, early efforts at some kind of agreement were constrained by lack of support and interest from the United States. Without the inclusion of the United States, any agreement on export credits would not have served to control the primary impetus for competition within the OECD, which was at that point the escalating challenge from the rebuilt industries of Europe to the dominant industries of the United States. The early-working Group on Export Credits and Credit Guarantees in the OECD was limited in its scope and was concerned primarily with the establishment of standard practices. During this period the United States was not sympathetic to agreements on limiting the terms and interest rates on export credits.[2] It enjoyed a favorable position resulting from low domestic interest rates and the ability to fund long maturities through Eximbank. Providing export financing competitive with the United States required subsidization by European governments to offset the advantage of lower rates and longer maturities. These early attempts at reaching an agreement did lead to the "understanding" on ship financing (to which the United States was not a party).

The U.S. position shifted in 1973-1974, when the oil embargo and the shake-up in the international financial system led to a general reconsideration of the role of export credits. In addition, U.S. interest rates began rising. The United States began to work actively for some agreed limitations on export credit terms. The reluctant parties proved to be the French and British. These countries sought to place strict limitations on maturity while keeping interest rates unconstrained. The United States argued for a strict interest floor of 8 percent while allowing maturities to reflect the life of the project or product.[3] The compromise that eventually was reached in 1976 entailed a lower interest rate floor of 7.25 to 8.0 percent, depending on the importer's level of development, and maximum maturities of 8.5 to 10 years. This "gentlemen's agreement" was formalized as the Arrangement on Guidelines for Officially Supported Export Credits in 1978.

Negotiations in the OECD have involved a process of consensus-building, which gives greater weight to individual country positions. Following a European Court of Justice ruling, the European Economic Community (EEC) members have negotiated as a group since 1975. This ruling has had the effect of requiring the formation of a common position in the EEC prior to negotiating with other OECD members, and has given the French effective veto power over the EEC. This has been an obstacle to change in the Arrangement. It has meant that countries benefiting from the status quo have been able to block adjustments to new international economic circumstances. As the United States has been the primary impetus for reform within the Arrangement, progress toward U.S. goals has been harder to achieve.

Many aspects of the OECD Arrangement have prevented it from effectively limiting the competitive use of export credits. To begin with, it is merely an agreement on standard terms and, until the most recent revisions, only provided for notification of financing offers in excess of those standards. Unlike the provisions of the various agreements of the Tokyo Round trade negotiations, it does not provide for retaliatory measures. The Exchange of Information is intended to facilitate the matching of below-scale credits as a retaliatory or countervailing action. However, the matching of below-scale offers, while a standard practice, has not served as a deterrent to concessionary financing. Mixed credits, or the blending of tied aid funds with export credits to yield a grant element of between 15 and 25 percent, are not adequately treated in the Arrangement. While the reporting requirements were improved for mixed credits in the October 1981 negotiations, there is still no consensus on standard treatment or practice. Compounding the problem, recent years have seen the proliferation of other export financing tools that fall outside the definitions of mixed credits but serve the same purpose (for example, through the provision of aid funds combined with private cofinancing).

The ability of the Arrangement to limit subsidization in export finance has also been severely constrained by the lack of an adjustment mechanism for the interest rate matrix and the lack of differentiation by currency. Beginning in 1976, interest rates rose to the point that the Arrangement rates were far out of line with market interest rates in countries such as the United States, France and Great Britain. In 1980, the Arrangement matrix was increased by 25-75 basis points; in 1981 an additional 225-250 basis point increase was agreed upon. This process of adjustment of minimum rates through periodic negotiation has not proved responsive to the U.S. goal of limiting subsidization. Each round of export credit negotiations has meant a new conflict of national interests in the OECD, with the result a belated compromise that reflects the leverage of those countries benefiting from the status quo.

In a study for the OECD conducted by Axel Wallen of Sweden, the alternative of a Differentiated Rate System (DRS) was proposed, along with a mechanism for automatic adjustment of a nondifferentiated system, or Uniform Moving Matrix (UMM).[4] The DRS would set export credit rates according to government bond rates for similar maturities in each currency, thereby directly relating export credit rates to market interest rates. The French objected, arguing that differences among national financial systems would prevent a fair comparison of market rates. The UMM would have a single matrix of rates for all currencies using special drawing rights (SDR) based weights, and would have the advantage of automatic adjustment, but not of differentiation by currency. The only result of these two proposals was the agreement on the minor increase in matrix interest rates in 1980. This rejection of automaticity in adjustment and differentiation by currency makes it likely that rates will continue to be set by periodic negotiation. In October 1981, there was a tacit acceptance of the principle of differentiated rates in the special rate accorded Japan because of its low market rates. This was extended in June 1981 to include an adjustment mechanism linking Japanese export credit rates to the long-term prime rate at a premium of 30 basic points. These developments were more of a compromise to keep Japan within the Arrangement than a movement toward adoption of an adjustment mechanism other than periodic negotiation, such as the DRS. However, if interest rates in other currencies fall significantly below Arrangement minimums, the adoption of similar mechanisms could lead gradually to a more widespread automaticity and differentiation by currency.

Two of the most important sectors in official export credits were left entirely outside the Arrangement: commercial aircraft and nuclear power plants. However, there has been progress in reaching an informal agreement with the Airbus partners. The United States was able to bring the Europeans up to its terms of a 12 percent interest rate and 42.5 percent cover in August 1981. Also, while not an ongoing agreement, the competing parties in bids for the Mexican nuclear power project were able to reach a "common line" on financing terms. Further similar attempts will likely be pursued by the United States. These developments suggest that a fruitful direction for negotiations would be the extension of sectoral agreements.

The current administration has based its export credit policy on the negotiation of agreements to reduce subsidies and neutralize financing as an element in international competition.[5] Through 1981 export credits and negotiating efforts received a high priority in U.S. trade policy. The immediate goals of the United States in the most recent round of negotiations which began in March 1982 were to restrict credits to the Soviet Union and secure a further increase in interest rates. Progress was achieved on both these grounds through a reclassification of countries and an increase of interest rates for the intermediate and relatively rich countries to 11.35 percent and 12.4 percent, respectively. By adopting the objective criterion of GNP per capita to govern the classification of countries, the Soviet Union and other Eastern Bloc countries were reclassified as relatively rich. The reclassification also will move a group of newly industrializing countries, which account for a large share of official export credits including Algeria, Brazil, South Korea, Taiwan, and Mexico, into the intermediate classification. In this manner the reclassification serves to increase average export credit rates in addition to the increase in the matrix.

Several other aspects of the most recent revisions of the OECD Arrangement also contribute to its strengthening. For the first time, the parties agreed not to derogate from the agreed terms, rather than merely issuing prior notification of below-scale credit offers. If this aspect of the new agreement holds it would represent a qualitative improvement in the discipline of the Arrangement. While it is still a "gentlemen's agreement," according it the status of a binding agreement will replace the inadequate mechanism of matching below-scale credit by competitors as the only source of discipline in the Arrangement. Also as part of this agreement not to break the new terms, members agreed not to offer mixed credits with a grant element of less than 20 percent. Whether this will control the use of mixed credits is questionable, but it is a step toward restricting their impact. In addition, the changeover to the new terms will be more clear-cut than in the past with a new limitation of six months on prior commitments for credits at the old Arrangement rates.

The development of export credit negotiations over recent years has seen progress toward U.S. goals in the OECD Arrangement. The United

States has always recognized the imperfect nature of the Arrangement but has compromised in acceding to it on the premise that it was a promising beginning and could be improved. Since 1976 the United States has concentrated on a strategy of steadily strengthening the Arrangement by raising interest rates, extending special sectoral agreements, seeking reclassifications, improving control over mixed credits, and moving to a market-based, differentiated interest rate matrix. Negotiating leverage to achieve progress in these areas has come from a variety of sources including linkage with other trade issues, pressure in other fora such as the General Agreement on Tariffs and Trade (GATT) and economic summit conferences, aggressive use of extension of maturities by Eximbank, and the threat of a much greater commitment of resources to Eximbank to neutralize foreign subsidies.

The status of export credit negotiations directly affects the Eximbank's policies. With the determination that other countries would not compromise on raising interest rates, the United States abandoned further negotiating efforts in 1979. The competitive posture of Eximbank was strengthened and the Bank became more aggressive. Since 1981 the Bank has pulled back from this posture by raising interest rates, but has used targeted derogation on maturity as an explicit tool to compete (with France in particular). While these derogations have been matched, this is more difficult for European credit agencies, and U.S. officials believe it has functioned as an effective "weapon." The competitive response of the Bank has been limited, even under Chairman Moore, and the idea of an aggressive Eximbank program that fully matches the financing available to competitors has only arisen as a threat to influence the negotiations.

Under its current policies and budget constraints, Eximbank clearly does not have the resources or financial flexibility to actively wage a competitiveness "war" aimed at forcing other countries into negotiation and meaningful compromise. It is not clear that the greater commitment to competitiveness in 1980 served that purpose. Despite proposed amendments to the Bank's charter emphasizing competitiveness, there does not exist a consensus in the government for the commitment of resources on a large scale to export credit subsidies with the purpose of influencing the negotiations. "War chest" bills providing such supplementary resources for the Bank have been approved in committee in both the House and Senate, but it was never clear that they were intended for actual implementation, except insofar as their approval in committee would send a signal to other countries that the United States was seriously considering this option.[6] Ambassador Brock has also proposed an "interest subsidy fund" to remove the stigma of Eximbank losses from its competitive stance, but this has not been developed into any concrete proposal.[7] Short of any such massive increase in the resources available to increase Eximbank's competitiveness, the ability of the Bank's competitive posture to serve as a tool in the current negotiating climate will be limited.

In spite of this recent progress made on strengthening the OECD Arrangement to control export credit competition and reduce subsidization, there are several fundamental characteristics of the OECD Arrangement that place limits on its ability to effectively eliminate export credit subsidization. These problems extend beyond the operational problems mentioned above. To begin with, in the context of negotiations within the OECD on export credits, there is no commitment to the elimination of subsidization except on the part of a few individual members such as the United States. There is no condemnation of the distortive effects of credit subsidies and no recognition of subsidized export credits as an unfair trade practice. The Arrangement is by its design a negotiated compromise between countries reliant on export credit subsidies and those that favor elimination of subsidies. For this reason it is unlikely to be an effective instrument or negotiating forum for the elimination of subsidies, which remains the basic objective of U.S. policy. As long as industrial competitors continue to use credit subsidies to promote capital goods exports, the best the United States may be able to achieve is a workable compromise on the level of subsidization.

Given the compromise on subsidization inherent in the OECD Arrangement, European differences with U.S. interest rate policy have also posed barriers to an effective export credit agreement. European resentment over high U.S. interest rates has grown steadily since 1979, and a change in U.S. interest rate policy was the most pressing matter, from the European perspective, at the most recent economic summit conference. The prevalent European attitude has been that high U.S. interest rates have in turn forced their monetary authorities to maintain higher interest rates than they otherwise would have. These higher European rates have been designed to stem outflows of capital to the United States as a result of interest rate differentials. In this environment of European resistance to U.S. monetary policy, resistance to an accord on export credit rates which accept high-dollar interest rates was also to be expected. As the level of interest rates in the Arrangement matrix has been the primary area of contention in export credit negotiations, this linkage to international financial issues has been a further deterrent to an effective agreement within the OECD. Rather than treating export credits strictly as a trade issue, their placement within the OECD under a special international agreement extends the discord over financial and general economic policies among the industrial countries.

Another fundamental problem with the OECD Arrangement is that its membership is limited and does not include the group of NICs. These countries, including Brazil, Korea, Taiwan, Mexico, and certain others in a more limited sense, are emerging as competitive exporters of capital goods. While their impact is limited, their importance will only increase in the future as their industrial capabilities and sophistication develop. The impact of the NICs is primarily in manufacturing plant exports in basic industries and in certain other industries such as shipbuilding (Korea) and commuter aircraft (Brazil). The commitment of this group of NICs to rapid industrial growth and the expansion of manufactured goods exports has meant strong government support for new industries through a range of promotional policies including export subsidies. In many cases, the success of a new industry is dependent upon penetration of export markets because of the limited size of domestic markets. Some NICs, such as Korea, have generally set export credit terms in line with the OECD Arrangement.[8] However, others, notably Brazil, have routinely subsidized export credits with no reference to the Arrangement and a very casual concern with credit worthiness.[9]

The problem posed by the emergence of the NICs as capital goods exporters is that they are unlikely to accede to an international agreement on export credits within the forum of the OECD. The OECD is typically regarded by developing countries, including the NICs, as a "rich men's club" where their interests cannot be effectively represented. It is unlikely that

NICs will enter into an OECD-based agreement on export credits for this reason. It is also unlikely that OECD members will accord the NICs any significant negotiating leverage to bring them into the OECD forum on export credit negotiations. The omission of the NICs may be a relatively minor concern in the current context of efforts to control export credit subsidization, yet is is a factor that will provide an additional impetus to export credit competition from outside the OECD Arrangement.

These factors, combined with the operational difficulties described above, will frustrate efforts to eliminate export credit subsidies. With continued negotiating success by the United States in the OECD, the Arrangement can be an effective forum to control export credit competition. This will allow Eximbank to offer competitive financing without the high subsidy levels of the past few years and without the resulting losses for the Bank. Continued U.S. efforts at strengthening the Arrangement, through the adoption of some means of interest rate adjustment to reflect changing financial market conditions, the extension of sectoral agreements, improved definitions and control of mixed credits, more effective enforcement of guidelines, etc., should bring further results. However, these results will necessarily be a negotiated compromise. Without a fundamental change of attitude on the part of France, England and others who consistently rely on subsidized export credit as a means of improving their international competitiveness, the gradual strengthening of the Arrangement will reach its limits. Indeed, several interview respondents involved in the OECD negotiations commented that the closer the negotiations came to seriously limiting subsidization, the greater the resistance was from France and England to making any further concessions.

Most of the negotiations on reform of the Arrangement have taken place in a context of rising interest rates. From 1978 to 1982 the increases in the Arrangement matrix lagged behind movements in market interest rates. In the current context of falling interest rates, it is quite feasible that market rates for a broad range of currencies will fall below the matrix rates to a significant degree. With a handful of countries below Arrangement rates, they may move increasingly toward straight loan guarantees at their domestic market rates, or press for special rates for official credit institutions as Japan has done. This would split the OECD members into two groups: those with full cover at market rates below the Arrangement, and those with subsidized rates at Arrangement levels. If market rates fall to a point to be significantly lower than the Arrangement for most countries, particularly for dollar rates, then there is likely to be pressure for a downward revision of the matrix. This will provide U.S. negotiators with the opportunity to play the obstructionist role and press for automaticity and differentiation in the interest rate matrix. However, even this outcome would not put the problem of subsidized export credit to rest. The willingness of competing nations to subsidize credits will persist, and any result is likely to be in the form of a negotiated compromise.

This tenacity on the use of export credit subsidies and resistance to international control contrasts with the accession to the GATT and the Subsidies Code Agreement. Unlike the OECD Arrangement, the Subsidies Code reflects the conviction that export subsidies, and even domestic subsidies with effects on trade, should not harm the industry of trading partners. Over the long run, the treatment of export credit subsidies under the Subsidies Code is the primary alternative to the OECD Arrangement, and could bring results more in line with U.S. goals of the elimination of subsidies.

INTERNATIONAL CONTROL OF EXPORT CREDITS:
THE SUBSIDIES CODE

The principal international agreement governing export subsidies is the Subsidies Code, negotiated as part of the Tokyo Round of Multilateral Trade Negotiations in 1979.[10] The Code states that while "subsidies are used by governments to promote important objectives of national policy," they can also have harmful effects on trade and production in other countries. The Code is intended to control the detrimental effects of subsidies through consultation, mediation, and the imposition of counter-vailing duties. An illustrative list of subsidies is included in the Code so as to clearly indicate the intended applications. Item K of the illustrative list specifically defines as a subsidy export credits granted by official institutions "at rates below those which they actually have to pay for the funds so employed (or would have to pay if they borrowed on international capital markets...)."[11] However, the second paragraph of Item K exempts export credits if they are granted on terms consistent with an international agreement on official export credits that at least 12 signatories have adopted. This exemption clearly sanctioned the separate treatment of export credit subsidies in the Arrangement and reaffirmed the OECD as the forum for international agreement on export credits. Hence, if it abandoned the Arrangement, the United States would have limited recourse to the Subsidies Code, depending on the interpretation of the exclusion in Item K.

The United States attempted to clarify these issues in 1981 by raising export credits with the Subsidies Code experts panel. Specifically, the sectors covered by "standstills" not limiting interest rates--aircraft and nuclear power--were suggested to be outside the exemptions in paragraph 2 of Item K. These actions were directed primarily at influencing the negotiations within the OECD, and did not receive substantive treatment in the GATT. Since the treatment of export credits in the Subsidies Code would be much more restrictive than that which has been negotiated in the OECD, the threat of such action is a credible one. Rather than just matching a competitor's terms--the standard means of offsetting credit subsidies envisioned in the Arrangement--Article 13 allows for direct countermeasures against the competitor upon the failure of consultation and mediation. The dissolution of the Arrangement would almost certainly bring about the treatment of export credits under the Code; the continuation of the Arrangment will limit the effectiveness of any unilateral action by the United States under the Code. Therefore, the negotiating strategy of simple recalcitrance--pursued primarily by France--has proved effective in limiting control of subsidization.

The Subsidies Code represents an attempt to control the impact of subsidies on trading patterns through codification and agreement on procedures and remedies. However, the Code confronts wide divergences among the GATT members in trade policy, economic structure and political philosophy. The United States has been much less inclined toward the use of subsidies to support and direct industry than its industrial counterparts. Europe and Japan have relied much more on an activist industrial policy in general, of which subsidization of certain industries is often a key element. A similar difference is apparent in government approaches to trade. The U.S. market has been more open to imports than most other industrial countries, and the U.S. government has not supported its exporters in overseas markets through the use of negotiating leverage or other promotional activities to the extent of its competitors. In this context, export credit subsidies are just one instrument of a trade and industrial policy intended to increase international competitiveness and expand domestic industry.

The constraints which the Subsidies Code and certain other of the MTN agreements are able to effect are limited in this environment: the Code is directed primarily at the most predatory types of market invasion assisted by government subsidy. To date, it has not been tested to any degree. However, the Subsidies Code and the MTN agreements in general represent an important extension of multilateral influence over aspects of government policy which have trade effects, even those which may be domestically oriented.[12] This expansion of multilateral control and standards of conduct has been singularly unmatched by any progress on export credits: paragraph 2 of Item K remains a gaping hole in the Subsidies Code.

As an international forum for the control and discipline of official export credits, the GATT and the clarifying Subsidies Code would not be subject to the fundamental obstacles that have plagued the OECD Arrangement. Most importantly, the basic agreement inherent in the Code is the elimination of the adverse effects of subsidies on trading partners. This contrasts with the balancing of national interests and negotiating leverage in the OECD over the degree of subsidy and the latitude for subsidization by individual countries. The ultimate defense against subsidized export credits under the Code would be direct retaliatory action against the offending nation. This course of action is reinforced by provisions of the Trade Agreements Act, such as Section 301, which allows firms affected by foreign government actions to request U.S. government action to seek the removal of the offending measure or to institute countervailing actions. The effectiveness of this type of direct retaliatory action as an enforcement mechanism is potentially much greater than the matching of competing financing offers. It affords U.S. industry the same level of protection against distortive measures by foreign governments in Third Country markets as the government affords in the U.S. market. The firm stand the United States is prepared to take regarding the impact of foreign subsidies in the U.S. market is currently illustrated by the careful consideration of the effects of foreign subsidies in steel and the imposition of countervailing measures. The extension of this same degree of resistance against other foreign subsidies to export credits would be facilitated through reference to the Subsidies Code. Treatment of export credits under the Code could also strengthen the Code over the long run by making it more inclusive in its coverage of trade subsidies.

This discussion line suggested that the Subsidies Code would provide a more effective forum for the strict control or elimination of export credit subsidies than the OECD Arrangement would. There are, of course, many problems with the GATT and the Subsidies Code. The Code has yet to be established as the major arbiter of the use of export subsidies; many recent countervailing actions on subsidies have been taken with reference to domestic trade legislation such as the U.S. action in subsidized steel imports. However, at the very least the threat of action under the Code can provide a negotiating lever to influence the OECD negotiations. The actual transference of international control of export credit subsidies to the Code, because of the exclusion in Item K of the Illustrative List, will depend on either the breakdown of the Arrangement or the emergence of a bloc willing to subject export credits to the potentially closer scrutiny inherent in the Code. For the immediate future, the imperfect, if improving, provisions of the OECD Arrangement will continue to permit the competitive use of subsidized export credit.

EXIMBANK: THE COMPETITIVE RESPONSE

In the absence of multilateral controls on export credits that effectively eliminate their competitive subsidization, the pressure of providing competitive finance will continue to dominate Eximbank policy, particularly if competitiveness is to be given greater weight in the Bank's charter. In the period 1979-1981, the disparity between interest rates in the Arrangement matrix and U.S. market rates, combined with the aggressive use of subsidized export credit by competitors, posed difficult problems for the Bank. Offering export finance competitive in rates and coverage with that of Europe and Japan meant a deepening negative spread on the Bank's current portfolio--the difference in interest rates on new loan commitments over the rate at which they were actually funded. The loans made during this period have now come to dominate the Bank's portfolio, causing net losses for the first time. At the same time, the increasing level of foreign subsidization brought on increased demand for Eximbank loans at competitive rates. The program limitations set by the Bank's budgetary authority proved to be increasingly constraining, and the Bank was forced to take measures to stretch its resources further and be more selective among competing loan requests.

Although Congress wishes to strengthen the competitiveness mandate of the Bank, neither has legislation been enacted or proposed, nor has Congress provided much guidance in terms of the problems competitiveness poses for the Bank. The degree of competitiveness is directly affected by the Bank's policy on incurring losses, which has ranged from an acceptance of losses in favor of greater competitiveness under Chairman Moore, to a commitment to restoring financial self-sufficiency under Chairman Draper. The "breadth" of competitiveness, or the coverage of Eximbank programs, is limited directly by the budget authority, but the criteria for selectivity among competing loan requests are a product of Bank policy. In structuring its programs, the Bank is continuously juggling between these conflicting measures and constraints.

There are several different means of interpreting the competitiveness mandate, each with different implications for Eximbank policy. The concept of neutralizing foreign credit subsidization as a factor in international competition is the most far-reaching in terms of the demands it would place on the Bank's programs. Strictly speaking, "neutralization" implies that the purchaser be faced with a choice between competing bidders which is indifferent to financing. The type of Eximbank program that would achieve this would require supporting any export that faces subsidized financing competition with an equivalent effective interest rate, equal maturity and coverage of other factors such as foreign and local costs. If the evaluation of financing terms by the importer were known, then terms would be modified, trading off one parameter for another to yield an equivalent level of subsidy so as to make the financing choice neutral. An extension of this approach would be to neutralize the effect of any foreign government intervention in export finance regardless of the subsidy element. This would mean the provision of programs equivalent to competitors' such as inflation insurance and foreign exchange risk insurance.

A lending program aimed at neutralization would be nonexclusive with respect to the type of export supported or other factors influencing an individual bidding situation. It would be comparable in breadth to the virtual entitlement programs offered by most European nations. Such a blanket approach to competitiveness would require a significant increase in Eximbank lending authority and, in the current interest rate climate, some means of financial support for the Bank. It does not imply the identical matching of nominal interest rates in other currencies, but the offering of an equivalent rate, perhaps at a similar discount from market rates. An approach based on neutralization of subsidies has been supported by industry groups in the United States, but the Bank has not had the resources necessary to implement such a broad-based response to foreign subsidization.[13]

A more restrictive interpretation of the role Eximbank should assume to be competitive is to offset the effects of foreign credit subsidies where financing is a relatively more important factor in competitiveness. This would imply an interest rate "close" to what would be equivalent to foreign offers, and coverage in other aspects which is roughly comparable. The resulting financing package would be similar enough to competitors' to ensure that subsidized financing was not the overriding influence on the sale. Such an approach would normally require directing resources to cases where financing is an important component of a bid, as is reflected in Eximbank's distinction of projects from products, and the use of unsubsidized rates or guarantees for other exports.

This approach is indicative of the competitiveness stance of the Bank under Chairman Moore. The Bank set interest rates and cover to yield a package within a range of the competition that would not greatly disadvantage the U.S. exporters' competitiveness. This type of strategy is facilitated by the existence of minimum terms as defined in the OECD Arrangement, for the Bank's terms could be standardized to be "close" to Arrangement terms. There is a widespread view at the Bank that being "close" means within roughly 100 basis points, and that a greater discrepancy in nominal interest rate will make an offer uncompetitive. With a large differential between U.S. government bond rates and Arrangement rates, this type of policy will still mean continued losses for the Bank. The experience of the Bank in 1979-1980 proved that even this more directed competitiveness policy will encounter resource constraints. With an extremely limited program authority for direct loans, the Bank's selection criteria will assume even greater importance with a wider differential between Eximbank rates and market rates. The industries or types of cases excluded from Eximbank support will have more to lose by not receiving direct loans, and would probably increase their lobbying efforts to influence case decisions and policies affecting loan criteria. This concept of offsetting foreign subsidized credit could be applied for any level of budget authority. However, in practice it is likely that the commitment to competitiveness implied by offering "offsetting" terms would be matched with budget authority sufficient to ensure a breadth of coverage across the most important cases.

A further limitation of competitiveness is also based on directing the Bank's resources to the types of cases where financing is most important, but refines this approach further to incorporate more case-specific factors. The current targeting approach of the Bank is based on this strategy. Examining all the factors that influence the sale, the Bank assesses the need for direct credit financing in an attempt to target those cases that would be lost without it. The Bank then also structures its financing offer to reflect the degree of support it judges is needed for the export to go through. In its concern over self-sufficiency, the Bank does not lower its interest rate to increase competitiveness. In this respect the Bank is not as responsive in terms of the degree of competitiveness as a purely offsetting policy would dictate. It will increase its cover from 42.5 percent to 65 percent, or 75 percent with supplier participation, as a means of lowering the effective rate to the borrower.[14] The Bank has also selectively offered to finance the 2 percent commitment fee in order to decrease its impact.

Under the current targeting approach, the most important tool for increasing the competitiveness of the Bank's financing has been the extension of maturities beyond that normally offered by competitors. This strategy draws on a particular strength of U.S. capital markets not easily matched by European competitors. It does constitute a unilateral derogation from Arrangement terms, but this was consistent with U.S. negotiating efforts over the past year. With the new terms entering into force, the United States will be bound by the Arrangement not to extend maturities and this will not be an option (barring a breakdown in compliance in general).

The targeting strategy is an attempt to yield the same outcome as the more systematic offering of competitive terms, but without the expenditure of resources on cases that would have gone ahead for reasons other than financing. That the Bank's standard terms were not competitive is evidenced by the fact that it relied on the extension of maturity to achieve competitiveness and that PC requests dropped off sharply following the increase in rates in July 1981. With the recent upward revisions in the Arrangement and the corresponding adjustment of Eximbank rates, the competitiveness of the Bank will be improved. The differential between Eximbank and Arrangement rates has been narrowed to 1 percent or less (except for Japan). The Bank's "Follow-up Studies" on PC dispositions have shown that there were a very small number of cases lost due to financing in the period prior to July 1981, when the Bank was within a similar range of the Arrangement matrix.[15] The Bank will continue to face resource constraints, however, which limit its breadth of competitiveness. With $3.7 billion proposed by the administration for direct loans in FY 1983, the Bank's targeting efforts will have to be even more exclusive. If, as in FY 1982, Congress partially restores cuts to Eximbank budget authority, the Bank would still be able to support only a declining share of capital goods exports, as inflation and increases in those exports raise their value.

The decrease in interest rate differentials, combined with increasing resource constraints, brings the Bank's targeting efforts to the fore of its competitive posture. In this respect, the reliance on individual case assessments as the primary means of targeting does not constitute a dependable, systematic response to the use of credit subsidies by competitors. The main problem with the Bank's targeting approach is the resulting lack of consistency and predictability.[16] An exporter must rely on the

Bank's assessment of his competitive situation and of the relative importance of factors influencing the sale. While the ability of the board and staff to evaluate individual cases may be quite good, a heavy reliance on individual case assessment does not promote consistency across cases. The Bank's staff has cited consistency and predictability as among the most important components of competitiveness in an export finance program.[17] This is particularly true as U.S. exporters are confronted with virtual entitlement programs supporting their competitors. Past Eximbank boards have, to a great degree, relied on the specific factors influencing each case to determine the need for Bank support and the level of that support as reflected in the structuring of the credit. For this reason, consistent adherence to policy guidelines has always been difficult to achieve at the Bank. The current board faces greater resource constraints on direct lending and has responded by institutionalizing its discretionary assessment process as a means of resource allocation. While the competitiveness of the Bank's standard terms is improved by the revisions in the Arrangement, these problems of resource targeting will remain.

The close alignment of Eximbank rates with Arrangement rates may ease concern over the competitiveness of standard Eximbank terms, but the problem of lack of differentiation by currency (excepting Japan) still affects the international comparison of interest rates. Countries with higher interest rates have more latitude for subsidization, while in Japan export credits are offered at a premium over the long-term prime rate. The usual standard of competitiveness utilized by the Bank, of being within 100 basis points of the Arrangement, and hence interest rates charged by competitors, thus does not take into account variations in market rates and thus the degree of subsidy among competitors. The reliance on a straightforward comparison of nominal interest rates is based in part on interest rate "illusion," or the preference of borrowers, particularly less-sophisticated developing countries, for lower nominal rates regardless of currency. Such straightforward comparisons ignore the linkage between nominal interest rates and exchange rate expectations. International movements of interest-sensitive short-term capital act to equilibrate the total return on investment resulting from interest and exchange rate appreciation/depreciation. Therefore, from the borrower's perspective, the relative debt service savings from lower nominal interest rates available in "hard" currencies will be offset, to a greater or lesser degree (depending on the accuracy of expectations), by currency appreciation. Most developing countries have now gained experience and sophistication in international borrowing, and are increasingly less prone to interest rate illusion. The advisory services of commercial and investment banks on the sourcing for large projects also contribute to accurate assessments of relative costs of borrowing in different currencies. These advisory services increasingly rely on long-dated forward contracts to convert effective interest rates into other currencies for a direct comparison. While the market in these long-dated forward contracts (over 5 years) is very thin, and current expectations (as expressed in the cost of forward cover) are not necessarily accurate predictors of future exchange rate movements, they do provide some basis for a comparison of the costs of potential borrowing in different currencies.

These factors suggest that interest rate illusion is not an important factor in an importer's financing decision. Preferences for borrowings in certain currencies may persist, for example, for purposes of overall debt management. However, it is not necessary for the Bank to "oversubsidize" to maintain its competitiveness by offsetting lower interest rate levels in other countries. In the current environment, the problem is not the competition from low interest rate export credits from Japan, but highly subsidized rates from France and England among others. Taking advantage of recent relaxations on foreign lending in Japan, Eximbank is currently encouraging guarantees of yen-denominated commercial bank loans as a means of supporting exporters in competition with Japan. The Bank is also exploring the possibility of funding loans directly in yen. These foreign currency denominated loans are clearly the best response to what amounts to competition among different capital markets.

The competitiveness of Eximbank, then, is not merely a question of the "closeness" of its terms to competitors and the level of its resources, but is also determined by the flexibility and innovativeness of its programs and the effectiveness of its allocation of resources. The commitment of resources necessary to fully "neutralize" foreign competition in export credits as described above would entail a much greater level of subsidization with probably marginal returns in terms of increased exports. The Bank's competitive response will, by the necessity of its resource constraints and the attitude of the current administration, be more limited. This does not mean that the Bank cannot be effective in responding to foreign credit subsidies, but that its effectiveness will depend on the careful design and implementation of its policies. The implications of the current policy orientation of the Bank for the support of U.S. industry in international trade, both in terms of offsetting the effects of foreign credit subsidies and in terms of linkages to other trade policy goals, follows in the next section.

IMPLICATIONS FOR TRADE POLICY

Project/Product Differentiation

The Bank's project/product distinction excludes a range of goods that are supported with subsidized finance by competitors. This has long been a criterion in the direct loan program, but is applied more restrictively at the present time. The distinction between project and product is not always clear, as the same types of goods can be involved in each. Machine tools may be exported as part of a turnkey factory project, exported separately as part of a multisourced project or sold individually. In the latter two cases, they would be confined to the supplier credit or discount loan programs. Similarly, many other types of equipment can be either part of a project or procured individually. The result is the inconsistent treatment of essentially similar exports. The inconsistency is even more marked because the Bank's medium-term supplier credit programs have consistently been the least competitive.[18] This results from a substantial degree of interest rate support by competitors, usually at the Arrangement minimum, whereas Eximbank offers only bank guarantees or discount loans. The most recent data on cases referred to the supplier credit programs show a distinctly higher portion of exports lost because of financing when referred to supplier credit programs.[19] Similarly, cases that were denied direct loan support but not referred to supplier credits because they were considered too large also fared poorly, especially to public buyers in developing countries.[20] Normally the discount loan program has served to partially fill this gap by refinancing commercial bank loans at an interest rate tied to the Federal Reserve Discount Rate. However, the maximum limit on discount loans was reduced to $2.5 million, creating a gap between that limit and the informal $5 million floor for direct loans. This measure was taken to reduce the demand for discount loans to within the budget ceiling and is presumably a temporary limitation. Yet further cuts are currently proposed for the discount loan program to $100 million, primarily because they are disbursed more rapidly and have an immediate effect on the Bank's borrowing requirements.

In terms of criteria for targeting resources effectively, the project lending distinction does serve to identify cases where financing is relatively more important. The specific criteria that constitute the distinction--a longer gestation period, large transaction size and long productive life--are indicative of the greater importance of financing in the importer's decisionmaking calculus. The fact that it has such a marked effect on the financing prospect of the excluded goods is a result of the lack of interest rate support in the medium-term programs. From the perspective of the exporter, it appears as an inconsistent and perhaps arbitrary distinction. In some cases exporters attempt to "bundle" products together in order to increase the value of the transaction to over $5 million and give it the appearance of a project. This type of response is indicative of the potential distorting effects resulting from the application of this criterion. The sharp distinction between the subsidies available in the direct loan program and the guarantees in medium-term programs mean that in practice it is proving to be particularly discriminatory in terms of the level of support available from the Bank.

Some type of program is desirable for capital goods that are on the borderline of the project and product distinctions. The discount loan program has been useful in this context and has been successful in the past in supporting these types of equipment exports, even at money market rates that are often high relative to competitors'. Although strict maintenance of the project/product criterion may be justified under the need to target scarce resources, some effort is needed to remove the distortions that this distinction causes. Specifically, the gap between the $2.5 million and $5 million transaction size should be filled. Expansion of the discount loan program would be perhaps the easiest means of removing the differential in the support of similar products between the direct loan and supplier credit/guarantee programs. Any measure to make medium-term programs more competitive, such as interest rate support, would involve an additional subsidy element. In addition to the exports lost, as evidenced by the Bank's follow-up studies, the arbitrary discrimination against borderline products/projects and the lack of competitiveness in medium-term programs also encourage a less-visible decrease in exports through overseas sourcing.

OVERSEAS SOURCING

The financing available for exports is a general preliminary consideration in a firm's competitive strategy. For a U.S.-based multinational firm with overseas production capability, the financing available from different countries is a factor in sourcing decisions to serve export markets in other countries. The overall competitive stance of official export financing systems will influence the planning process and a firm's sourcing proposals in competitive bidding situations. It is difficult to estimate the extent of overseas sourcing to serve Third Country markets due to financing considerations. These are internal corporate decisions subject to multiple factors. Assuming profit-maximizing behavior, a consistent differential in financing terms will lead to a marginal reallocation of production to take advantage of more favorable financing. The cost of overseas sourcing is lower for a firm with existing manufacturing capacity in other countries than in the case where significant new investment would be required. It is among well-established multinationals that export credit terms will then have a proportionally greater effect on sourcing decisions. For these firms the incremental costs in terms of managerial problems, start-up costs, retooling costs, etc., will be lower. However, there is likely to be some effect even on new investment aimed at production for export, as financing terms will be one element in the investment assessment and will affect pricing decisions. Liberal export credit terms are a standard incentive offered by industrializing countries attempting to attract foreign investment.

There are several aspects of Eximbank's competitive stance that will act to encourage overseas sourcing. Resource constraints force the exclusion of certain cases from direct loan support that will lead firms to utilize other production bases with more liberal export credit programs. The exclusion and inconsistent treatment of products in the direct loan program, as suggested above, will influence sourcing decisions for that class of goods. The lack of consistent and dependable support for a firm's products, exemplified in the Bank's discretionary assessment of individual cases, has led some firms to submit duplicate bids from U.S. and foreign sources and also to source directly overseas. The more straightforward lack of competitiveness in medium-term programs is perhaps the greatest encouragement to overseas sourcing. This class of products, representing mostly self-contained machinery and equipment, is of a small enough scale to allow the establishment of multiple production facilities. This is clearly much less true of larger "big-ticket" project-related equipment such as aircraft and electric power machinery. Clearly, the demonstration by a country of commitment to aggressive export financing is only one of a group of considerations that affect sourcing decisions. Export credit terms are likely to play some role, however, in the transfer of production overseas.

Limited empirical evidence on overseas sourcing to take advantage of liberal export credit facilities does exist in a recent survey by the Machinery and Allied Products Institute (MAPI).[21] The MAPI survey revealed that 14 firms out of the 39 surveyed reported 39 transactions diverted to foreign affiliates exclusively or primarily because of export financing terms in 1981. The total value of the diverted sales was $386.7 million, which was sourced in Canada ($169.45 million), France ($97.5 million), Japan ($39.7 million), Spain ($24.45 million), the U.K. ($23.41 million), Netherlands ($21.5 million), Brazil ($10.23 million) and Belgium ($.5 million). In addition, nine companies reported they had lost or not bid on projects totaling $4.3 billion because of uncompetitive financing.

The MAPI survey is of limited value for several reasons. There is no indication of what percentage, either of total exports or of total exports that could potentially be sourced overseas, the reported transactions constituted for the firms surveyed. Hence, there is no means of attaching any relative importance to the absolute figure of $386.7 million. There is also no indication of the relation of the sample of firms to the population of capital goods exporters, other than that they were all firms with active foreign affiliates and did not include aircraft and nuclear power manufacturers. There is no indication of the controls or verification procedures used (if any) to prevent the reporting of biased or inaccurate data. This is particularly important because the survey was obviously intended for the advocacy of MAPI's interest and support of lobbying efforts for a larger Eximbank budget. There is also no identification of the specific aspect of noncompetitive export financing (interest rate differentials, denial of direct credit support, etc.) that led the reporting firms to source their exports overseas. Nevertheless, in spite of these shortcomings, the survey is important in that it demonstrates that some degree of overseas sourcing does exist in response to export credit terms. More rigorous research efforts of this type will no doubt continue to define the extent and nature of overseas sourcing, which otherwise goes largely undetected by Eximbank and other agencies in their monitoring and policy analysis functions.

The impact of overseas sourcing extends beyond the immediate loss of exports for the United States. Factors that influence the transfer of production overseas have effects on U.S. competitiveness and trade patterns in more subtle ways. Here again, export financing is just one element among many, but the fact that it does operate to induce overseas sourcing in capital goods means that it is a factor in inducing a more rapid transfer of technology abroad than would otherwise have taken place. The U.S. strength in manufactured goods exports, both overall and to developing countries, has been in more advanced higher-technology goods.[22] The product life cycle theory of international trade suggests that new products are initially produced in the home country, at the site of the firm's major production and R&D centers, and intended primarily for the domestic market. Export markets are also served initially from this home production base. As the technology becomes standardized, production then shifts overseas to serve foreign markets where the firm at that point faces competition. Ultimately, production for the U.S. market may also shift to lower-cost countries. Many factors have changed to reduce the applicability of the product life cycle theory as a determinant of U.S. export patterns.[23] Firms now usually plan new products with global markets in mind from the outset, and established multinational production networks of major firms facilitate global sourcing strategies. The United States also does not command the technological lead it had in the postwar period through the 1960s, and the factor cost characteristics of the industrial nations have converged. However, the product life cycle theory does still retain some validity for new, technology-intensive products such as certain types of capital goods. Increased overseas sourcing of these goods in response to noncompetitive export financing will shorten the time period during which they are produced in the United States, thus "speeding up" the product life cycle development. The distortive effects of foreign credit subsidies, thus, also extend, through their influence on overseas sourcing, to patterns of production and trade that have been a major determinant of U.S. competitiveness.

Support for High-Technology Industries

Technological innovation, as suggested by the previous discussion, is a major determinant of industrial competitiveness. The United States has consistently supported its leading high-technology industries through incentives for innovation and government programs and expenditures to stimulate research and development. In trade policy, the United States has concentrated on efforts to remove barriers to trade in high-technology goods, for example, in raising the issue as a matter of special concern on the agenda of the 1982 GATT Ministerial meetings. Barriers to trade in high-technology goods involve various means of protecting domestic markets through government procurement practices, restrictive technical standards, subsidization, etc., and of promoting exports through the use of subsidized export credits, diplomatic leverage and other promotional tactics. As was outlined in Chapter 3, the capital goods sectors are in general technology-intensive, and several industries in particular whose exports are typically financed through official credits may be classified as high technology. These would include satellite communications systems, telecommunications equipment in general, aircraft and aircraft engines, numerically controlled machine tools, robotics and other automated manufacturing equipment, and certain types of electrical equipment.

As part of an articulated industrial policy of government support for these industries in Western Europe and Japan, subsidized export credits are virtually assured where securing export markets is an objective. The level of support these industries receive in other countries generally exceeds that prevailing in the United States. Often this is rationalized under "infant industry" arguments, as is the case in the French electronics industry. Concerted French efforts to capture developing country markets in telecommunications equipment is one example where export credits have played an important role as a means of official support.

Conversely, the current targeting efforts of Eximbank have centered on identifying industries with a significant technological advantage as not needing subsidized credit to compete with their inferior, but officially financed, counterparts. This targeting rationale is based on the role that financing plays in international competition: it is relatively more important when goods are less differentiated by performance characteristics or technical superiority. The sale of U.S. satellite communications equipment to Australia cited earlier is a good example of the successful application of this criterion: the sale went ahead without direct credit support in the presence of subsidized credit competition based on the technical superiority of U.S. equipment. However, targeting direct credit support to exclude those U.S. firms or industries with a significant technological advantage has the potential of risking a loss of important markets should the Bank mistake the relative importance of financing to the sale. Should this occur, the effect would be to encourage the catching-up efforts of competitors that are facilitated by the aggressive use of export credits.

The Bank does attempt to monitor these industries and cases, and is alert to any signals that may suggest a U.S. firm no longer has command of its industry internationally. Through its monitoring of the competitive environment in export credits, the Bank staff and board are aware of the predatory use of export credits to capture new markets, and will be quick to respond to competitive threats. While some have suggested that the lack of aggressive Eximbank financing of leading U.S. industries invites foreign competition, it is doubtful that over the long run consistent direct credit support would deter foreign competitors from attempting to enter new markets. The problem in pursuing this targeting strategy lies in the determination of the critical period or specific cases where foreign subsidized financing will make the difference in market penetration.

Eximbank finance is an important factor in support of high-technology exports because of the use of credit subsidies by competitors to support their high-technology industries. The Bank's role is in offsetting these credit subsidies, as in other industries. The Bank would be an inefficient means of attempting to offset the effects of extensive government support of high-technology industries by other industrial nations. If additional government intervention is necessary in this regard it would be better directed at the source of technological advancement through greater incentives for innovation and increasing research and development effort.

Government Intervention in Support of Exports

As the preceding discussion of high-technology industries illustrates, U.S. capital goods producers are often faced with competition from foreign industries that receive extensive governmental backing. Where government support takes the form of outright subsidy (except export credits), overly restrictive government procurement preferences, and other blatantly protectionist means, some form of remedy is generally available through provisions of the U.S. Trade Acts or the MTN codes. However, government support often takes less tangible or easily countered forms. A particular problem U.S. firms face from European industry is that of competition from state-owned enterprises. This is especially true in aircraft and aircraft engines, nuclear power, and telecommunications. State-owned enterprises are typically not under the same type of pressure to produce continual profits as is private industry in the United States, and typically respond more to the goals of increasing production and employment. They are in many cases more willing to take loss-leading ventures into new markets than their U.S. counterparts are.

While state-owned firms typically enjoy a variety of government supports, they also share these with private firms that are the favored targets of industrial policies. The use of negotiating leverage by high-level government officials and a willingness to introduce diplomatic concessions into commercial negotiations are perhaps the most distortive of these measures. One example of the extreme use of these types of linkages was the tying of aircraft sales to the granting of reciprocal landing rights. The recognition of the distortive effects of these practices led to the civil aircraft agreement concluded in the Tokyo Round of multilateral trade negotiations. In general, the United States has been more reticent than competitors to utilize such means of export promotion. For example, high-level visits by U.S. officials to foreign countries are rarely accompanied by commercial representatives of U.S. firms, which is a standard practice of other industrial nations.

In the past, the United States could afford to ignore these practices because of the dominance of U.S. industry in world markets. The gradual erosion of this dominance in many industries has increased the need to respond to these types of intervention by foreign governments. The issue confronting Eximbank is what its role will be in this response. At present the Bank is in many cases the only tangible form of U.S. government support for industries confronted by these types of competitive pressures. Is the Bank to be the primary means of supporting U.S. firms against the pricing flexibility of foreign state-owned companies? Should the Bank be "unleashed" to counter excessive diplomatic support or linkage to other types of foreign policy concessions to which the United States is unwilling to respond in kind?

To date the Bank has not assumed these roles to any significant degree. To do so would mean a reorientation of the Bank from countering export credit competition, and would no doubt further strain the decision-making process at the Bank by adding to its already conflicting mandates. What is needed is the close coordination of the Bank with other export promoting activities of the U.S. government. Without the Bank becoming a subordinate of the agencies responsible for trade promotion, more visible cooperation would improve relations both with foreign buyers and domestic business constituencies.

Support for Service Industries

The transformation of the U.S. economy to a service-based economy has been developing throughout the postwar period, and has intensified in the past decade with the shift of manufacturing industries to developing countries. Services exports have become an increasingly important component of the U.S. current account. Service industries face a number of barriers to open competition in most countries. U.S. support of services exports has become an important trade policy issue, exemplified by the efforts to bring international trade in services under the same set of principles governing trade in products. However, in the industrial project-related fields of engineering, U.S. exporters typically do not get the same degree of support, either through foreign assistance or official financing, as they do in other industrial countries. Eximbank has experimented with the financing of feasibility studies and other engineering/construction services in the past, but does not do so explicitly at the present time under the rationale of targeting its resources to actual product exports. Nevertheless, a significant component of project exports represents services. The construction of large infrastructure projects typically requires a great degree of site-specific engineering and design, as well as the services involved directly in the construction. The Bank does not, however, monitor or vigorously examine the extent of its support of service industries through project financing.

The United States does provide financing and assistance specifically for feasibility studies through the Trade Development Program (TDP) administered by AID. The importance of supporting feasibility studies is that the firm conducting the study plays a significant role in the final design of the project, and thus in the equipment selected. In many cases this means that procurement for the project will be sourced from the home country of the firm, so that the final export sales, often coming several years later, are influenced strongly by the initial contract for the feasibility study.

The issue facing Eximbank is, again, what role it will play in the financing of project-related services such as feasibility studies. The transaction size of feasibility studies for most projects is small relative to Eximbank direct loans, and explicit support of these studies would require a relaxation in direct lending criteria. The Trade Development Program is relatively small, with a program budget of only $5 million for FY 1982. The experience of the Bank staff in industrial project financing suggests that such a program may be better administrated and more efficiently sponsored at the Bank itself. The Trade Development Program had its origins in providing technical assistance in countries where foreign aid was being phased out, and thus was logically connected with AID. With its primary focus today on financing feasibility studies to promote U.S. exports, it would benefit from being directly connected to Eximbank, or perhaps the Commerce Department Office of Major Projects in the International Trade Administration (ITA). At the very least, the administration of the TDP could benefit from an exchange of personnel between AID and Eximbank.[24]

The current trade policy initiatives on services exports so far have not moved Eximbank policy toward explicit support for services exports. The competitive financing environment in feasibility studies suggests a stronger role for the Bank which is directly related to project finance, either through its own programs or in conjunction with TDP.

Subsidized Export Credits in the U.S. Market

Foreign subsidized credits not only affect U.S. export industries, but also offset sales in the U.S. market. Unlike Eximbank policy of avoiding direct credit support for exports to other industrial countries, many other countries are willing to support capital goods exports with subsidized credits with little reference to destination. Due to high domestic interest rates over the past three years, the financing terms available from foreign export credit agencies have often proved especially attractive to U.S. purchasers. For example, the 8 percent dollar financing available from Brazil for purchases of commuter aircraft aided the Bandeirante's penetration into the U.S. market.[25]

The United States has pressed for a limitation over subsidized credits into other industrial country markets in the export credit negotiations in the OECD in an effort to control their impact on the U.S. market. This effort was largely successful in the over 1 percent interest rate increase in the Arrangement rates for relatively rich countries agreed to in July 1982.[26] The U.S. government has also made commitments actively resisting the use of subsidized foreign credits in the U.S. market. This commitment transcends the minimum rates stipulated in the OECD Arrangement, as it would extend to credit offers made at Arrangment rates, which still represented a subsidy relative to domestic interest rates. As even the 12.4 percent Arrangement rate is below current prime and corporate bond rate levels, latitude for subsidization exists and could bring on retaliatory action from the United States.

Export credits in the U.S. market directly affect Eximbank because of the provision in the 1978 Amendments for Eximbank financing of U.S. suppliers facing subsidized financing competition in domestic sales. The Bank is one of the means of taking countervailing actions. The stipulation was invoked in the recent contract award by the New York City Metropolitan Transit Authority (MTA) to Bombadier of Canada for mass transit railcars. Budd, the U.S. bidder, requested a loan from Eximbank to counter the 9.7 percent financing offered by Canada's Export Development Corporation. Secretary Regan, however, declined to authorize the Bank to consider the case on the grounds that the award would have gone to Bombadier in any case because of other considerations including a prompter delivery schedule, greater New York State content, and a desire on the part of the MTA to diversify its sources. Budd is continuing this case with the International Tariff Commission (ITC), which is giving careful consideration to the contract award and the subsidized financing. The ITC has made a preliminary determination that the Canadian credit subsidy may have caused economic damage to U.S. industry, but the final outcome is not yet clear.

The strong stand by the United States on the use of credit subsidies in the domestic market contrasts with the more patient negotiating efforts on export credits, in general, in the OECD. This response is mandated by legislation governing unfair trade practices and, of course, facilitated by direct means of control over the purchaser. In the event of a counter-vailing action against a foreign credit offer that is within Arrangement terms yet subsidized by U.S. interpretation, the action may be viewed by competitors as reneging on the Arrangement. However, a firm stand--even one resulting in damage to relations within the OECD concerning export credits--would be consistent with the U.S. effort to control and eliminate the continued use of export credit subsidies.

Subsidization of Industrial Capacity

The longer-run effects of competitive export credit subsidization present related trade policy problems through the creation of excess capacity in certain basic industries. Capital goods exports serve to build industries in other nations, supplying the productive machinery, plant, equipment and infrastructure for industrializing nations. These imports are typically financed with official export credits on subsidized terms. The more advanced developing countries in particular have been large importers of capital goods from the industrial countries. The establish-ment of basic industries has often been the cornerstone of these countries' development strategies. In addition to supplying their domestic markets, tapping the large potential markets in the industrial countries has become an objective. In some cases these industries are uneconomic, and are maintained through subsidization and protection for their perceived valued in promoting industrialization.

In the industrial countries, these basic industries are mature and well established, and often enjoy a high degree of government support and protection. The adjustment to changing patterns of global production and comparative advantage has been slow and painful, resulting in the mainten-ance of capacity beyond what would have been maintained under more open competition. The combination of rapid industrial expansion in the develop-ing countries and slow adjustment in the industrial countries has created global surplus capacity in certain basic industries. Steel is perhaps the best example of this situation; the excess capacity, subsidization, and protec-tion in the steel industry have created one of the thorniest trade problems in recent years.

The easy financing terms available for the importation of new steel mills is not, of course, the primary cause of the expansion of steel capacity. The major reason is the dedication of many countries to the development or maintenance of steel industries. The subsidized financing terms available do, however, add fuel to the fire and are an additional factor influencing the expansion of the industry. The issue is not to control or otherwise limit plant exports in industries suffering from overcapacity: this would merely be another means of protection. The problem lies in the continuing subsidization of those plant exports through officially supported credits.

Eximbank cannot unilaterally affect this issue by withholding credits for steel mills or other industries plagued with overcapacity. Competitors would still finance and build the new plants. However, these industries do constitute a suitable area for special sectoral agreements to limit subsidization. In addition to steel, chemicals and petrochemicals are also beginning to exhibit chronic overcapacity. One industry which was the subject of the first sectoral agreement in the OECD is shipbuilding, in which surplus capacity continues to exist, largely because of protective subsidies. In the current volatile environment in the steel industry, an accord on steel plant exports in unlikely. Nevertheless, the existence of overcapacity aggravated by subsidized export credits will continue to pose trade policy problems in an increasing number of industries.

NOTES

1.   OECD, cited in "Foreign Export Subsidies," Electronic News (October 12, 1981).

2.   Joan Pearce, Subsidized Export Credit, Chatham House Papers, No. 8, 1980, p. 43.

3.   GAO Report, "To Be Self-Sufficient or Competitive?" (June 1981), p. 22.

4.   OECD, "Implications for the Arrangement of Operational Alternatives to the Present Matrix," Report by Mr. Wallen, 1980.

5.   Testimony of John Lange on Eximbank Budget Authorization before the subcommittee on International Trade, Investment and Monetary Policy of the House Committee on Banking, Finance and Urban Affairs, April 28, 1981.

6.   U.S. Congress, Competitive Export Financing Act of 1981, 97th Cong., 1st sess., S. 868 and H.R. 3228.

7.   Testimony of William Brock before the subcommittee on Trade, House Ways and Means Committee, October 28, 1981.

8.   IMF Survey, November 29, 1979, p. 369.

9.   "Brothers in Misery," Forbes (April 12, 1982), pp. 45-46.

10.   GATT, "Agreement on Interpretation and Application of Articles VI, XVI and XXIII of the General Agreement on Tariffs and Trade" (1979).

11.   Ibid., p. 39.

12.   Richard Blackhurst, "The Twilight of Domestic Economic Policies," The World Economy, Vol. 4 (1981), p. 358.

13.   For example, the "Recommendations" of U.S. Chamber of Commerce, "Statement on Competitive Export Financing," November 11, 1981.

14.   For example, if private financing were available at 16 percent, the extension of cover from 42.5 percent to 65 percent would decrease the blended annual rate from 14 percent to 12.9 percent. The commitment fee would increase because of the increased loan amount. However, the rate charged by the participating institution would probably be lower because of the shorter term of the private loan.

88

15. U.S. Export-Import Bank, Policy Analysis Staff Memorandum, "Semi-Annual PC Follow-Up," November 16, 1981.

16. Frustration with the Bank's decisionmaking procedures led one interview respondent to suggest that it would even be better if loans were allocated on a first-come, first-served basis until the budget authority ran out.

17. U.S. Export-Import Bank, Policy Analysis Memorandum, "A Policy Posture for a Now and Future Competitive Eximbank," July 10, 1979.

18. U.S. Export-Import Bank, Report to the Congress on Export Credit Competition and the Export-Import Bank of the United States, October 1980; January 1980.

19. U.S. Export-Import Bank, Policy Analysis Staff, "Follow-up on Cases Denied Direct Loan Support," November 1981, p. 2.

20. Ibid., p. 2.

21. Machinery and Allied Products Institute, Survey of Selected Member Companies Concerning Export Financing, March 1982.

22. Raymond Mikesell and Mark G. Farah, U.S. Export Competitiveness in Manufactures in Third World Markets" (Washington: Georgetown University Center for Strategies and International Studies, 1980), pp. 94-95.

23. Raymond Vernon, "The Product Life Cycle Theory Reconsidered," Oxford Bulletin of Economics and Statistics 41 (1979).

24. A common criticism by private sector interview respondents was that AID personnel in the Trade Development Program are not as well attuned to commercial considerations as their counterparts at the Eximbank or Commerce.

25. "The Plane that Flies on Financing," Business Week (April 12, 1982), p. 46.

26. This effort was to an equal or greater extent to control credits to the Eastern bloc, which in the reclassification moves to the relatively rich category.

6
Major Foreign Programs and Policies for Financing Exports

OVERVIEW

Faced with similar technologies from competing exporters, a foreign purchaser will often select the bidder that offers the best financing. Table 6.1 highlights the amount and share of official export credits in 1978 by the United States and its four major competitors.

As noted in Chapter 5, OECD members agreed in 1977 on an "Arrangement on Guidelines for Official Supported Exports Credits" to avoid the dangers of competitive underwriting of official financed interest rates. Despite the Arrangement, however, the dangers of an export credit war loom prominently, largely because of different interpretations of the guidelines that individual members employ; the temptations to stimulate exports to cushion the effects of recession make the prospects of a comprehensive settlement tenuous at best.

A comparative assessment of U.S. Eximbank's activities with those of its major competitors indicates that despite Eximbank's efforts to match its competitors, a number of constraints prevent the Bank from offering competitive financing for U.S. exports. As Table 6.2 reveals, the percentage of total exports officially supported by loans, insurance and guarantees is far higher in other industrial countries than in the United Sates. While these figures include nonloan activities, they do indicate greater government commitment to exports than exists in the United States. This commitment is reflected in a number of specific areas:

Interest Rates

Table 6.3 compares the effective cost of interest rates to the borrower charged by the United States and its four major competitors for a government-supported, long-term loan to finance an export to a developing country. Because of the large values of most long-term transactions, it is in this area that competition has been most keen, although the mechanisms for providing long-term financing vary between countries. While Eximbank relies principally on fixed-rate loans and/or guarantees, other countries, such as France, rely on a variety of instruments--subsidized loans and guarantees, preferential refinancing to commercial banks--while others, such as Germany, principally use a guarantee system. Despite the different approaches taken by various governments, the intent is to provide the lowest possible interest rates to the borrower. See Table 6.4 for a comparison of official export credit regimes.

TABLE 6.1
Official export credits exceeding five years - 1978: regional distribution
(export value in millions of dollars)

	West						Share of Total Credits				
	France	Germany	Japan	U.K.	U.S.	Total Five Countries	France	West Germany	Japan	U.K.	U.S.
Africa/Middle East	40%	27%	17%	8%	20%	$ 3,137	39%	22%	12%	3%	25%
(North Africa)						(1706)	(35)	(14)	(10)	--	(42)
(Other)						(1431)	(44)	(31)	(14)	(6)	(5)
Asia/Oceania	17%	9%	29%	58%	42%	$ 3,701	14%	6%	17%	18%	45%
(Japan/Australia/ New Zealand)						(149)	--	(17)	--	--	(83)
(Other)						(3552)	(14)	(6)	(18)	(19)	(43)
Europe/Canada	35%	40%	33%	24%	23%	$ 3,955	27%	25%	18%	7%	22%
(Developing Western Europe and Canada)						(1002)	--	(12)	(19)	--	(68)
(Developing Western Europe)						(309)	(49)	(7)	(6)	(4)	(34)
(East Europe)						(2644)	(35)	(32)	(19)	(10)	(4)
Latin America	9%	24%	20%	11%	14%	$ 2,004	14%	30%	22%	6%	28%
TOTAL 1978:	$3086	$2516	$2149	$1164	$3882	$12,797	24%	20%	17%	9%	30%
	100%	100%	100%	100%	100%						

Source: Eximbank Report to Congress, January 1980.

TABLE 6.2
Percentage of total exports supported by loans, insurance and guarantees

Country	Exports as % of GNP	Total Official Insurance, Guarantees & Loans as % of Total Exports[a]	Officially Supported Long-Term Export Credits as % of Total Exports	Officially Supported Long-Term Export Credits as % of Manufactured Goods Exports
Japan	12%	35%	2.2%	2.2%
U.K.[b]	20%	35%	1.6%	2.0%
France[b]	17%	29%	3.9%	5.2%
West Germany	23%	12%	1.8%	2.0%
U.S.	7%	6%	2.7%	4.2%

Source: GAO Report, ID-80-16.

[a]All countries except the United States require an exporter to obtain commercial and political risk insurance as a condition for obtaining a government-supported loan. The chart excludes exports financed with foreign assistance funds. The U.S. estimate also excludes exports financed by the Commodity Credit Corporation and the Foreign Military Credit Sales program. Estimates for other countries may include small amounts of military and agricultural exports supported by their export credit agencies.

[b]Estimate based on June 30, 1978 data.

TABLE 6.3
Medium-term fixed export credit interest rates (percent)

	Nominal			Effective[a]		
	1979	1980[b]	1981[c]	1979	1980	1981
France	7.25	7.37	8.00	8.00	8.12	8.75
West Germany	7.50	8.62	9.25	8.30	9.42	10.05
Japan	7.25	7.37	9.25	7.85	7.97	9.85
United Kingdom	7.25	7.37	8.00	7.85	7.97	8.60
United States	11.08	13.08	16.04[d]	a) 11.33[e]	13.33	17.05
				b) 12.58	14.58	18.30

Source: U.S. Export-Import Bank, Report to the U.S. Congress on Export Credit Competition, December 1982.

[a]Face rates are adjusted upward to effective rate by accounting for insurance, guarantee, and commitment fees in the following amounts: France (.75), Germany (.80), Japan (.60), and the United Kingdom (.60).

[b]Nominal rates for 1980 are the approximate averages of the rates charged before and after the Arrangement change in July 1980.

[c]Nominal rates for 1981 are Arrangement rates for intermediate countries with no adjustment for the Arrangement change in November 1981.

[d]U.S. nominal rate for 1981 assumes a 65/20 Eximbank/commercial bank financing package (with a 15 percent cash payment). Eximbank portion at average discount rate of 15.04 percent plus 1 percent markup by the bank plus a commitment fee of 0.25. Commercial bank portion at 19.25 percent, which was the average bank rate for industrial and commercial loans in 1981.

[e]Line a) represents the effective rates assuming only a 0.25 percent discount loan commitment fee. Line b) assumes a 0.25 percent discount loan commitment fee plus a 1.25 percent fee for the optional insurance.

As Table 6.3 indicates, the major competitors of the United States provide base financing at the floor of the OECD Arrangement. The base rate represents the blended government and commercial rates that are generally combined in an export financing package; the costs of required fees and insurance are included so as to accurately compare the interest rates offered between countries. While the comparative rates suggest that the United States offers the least-competitive nominal rates, the rates do not include the effect of differential exchange rate trends; the differential between rates offered by the United States and Germany, for example, may at times be offset by fluctuations in the value of the dollar against the deutsche mark (DM).[1]

Interest rates offered by major competitors to the United States for intermediate-term financing reflect a similar pattern. As Table 6.5 illustrates, France, Italy, Japan and the United Kingdom offered medium-term government supportive loans at rates between 7.75 and 8.1 percent; these countries attempt to keep the interest rate charged to the borrower at the minimum allowed by the Arrangement.[2]

Although most German medium-term loans come from the private sector, a system of government loan guarantees and preferential financing from the Bundesbank allows the Ausfuhrkredit-Gmbh (AKA) consortium of commercial banks to offer rates approaching official rates. Similarly, Eximbank does not itself offer medium-term financing, providing instead support to commercial banks through guarantees by the Federal Insurance Contributions Act (FICA), its discount loan program, or its Cooperative Financing Facilities; but unlike Germany, the effective interest rate to the borrower is several percentage points above its competitors.

Mixed Credits

One vehicle France, the United Kingdom and Japan have employed to lower the cost of financing below the Arrangement floor has been the selective use of mixed export credits and development assistance funds for those projects of "national importance." France is the most frequent user --or abuser--of mixed credits. Despite criticisms from the United States that the practice is an "artificial and counterproductive export stimulus," France has increased the volume and magnitude of mixed credit projects; in 1978, France granted 18 new mixed credits, financing a total export value amounting to $1 billion, with the concessionary aid portion amounting to $195 million. Because the aid portion carried a very low interest rate-- 3.5 percent--and long repayment terms--20 to 30 years--the incentive is alluring. Sectors supported by French mixed credits include communications, transportation, and agriculture as well as general purpose credit lines to be used for financing medium-sized capital goods and equipment purchases. The United Kingdom has withdrawn from a plan to limit mixed credit offers to transactions involving similar French offers and instead has set up mixed credits that include 30 percent foreign assistance, payable over 25 years at 2-4 percent. Although Japan claims it does not employ mixed credits, Japanese foreign aid funds are used to finance natural resource projects in developing countries where the output is exported to Japan. Although these aid funds are untied to procurement of Japanese equipment and services, critics charge that orders for Japanese firms are a condition for obtaining the aid. An Eximbank study noted that from March 1978 to March 1979, U.S. firms lost two sales--despite Eximbank backing-- to Japanese firms who could provide concessionary aid financing.

TABLE 6.4 Comparative export credit financing regimes

	Canada	France	West Germany	Italy	Japan	U.K.	U.S. Commercial	U.S. Noncommercial
Percent coverage								
Supplier	100 maximum	80-90 commercial risks; 95 political risks	80, 85 or 90 (Hermes)		90	90-95 normally	85-100	70-90
Buyer	100 maximum	95	80, 85 or 90 (Hermes)		90	100	85-100	70-90
Official export credit institution	Export Development Corporation (EDC)	COFACE, Banque Francaise du Commerce Exterieur (BFCE)	Hermes, Kreditanstalt fur Wiederaufbau (KfW)	Sace, Mediocredito	Japanese Eximbank MITI Department	Export Credit Guarantees (ECGD)	Eximbank	
Financing & refinancing arrangements			Ausfuhrkredit-Gmbh (AKA), a consortium of commercial banks				Private Export Funding Corporation (PEFCO)	
Bank pools			Member commercial banks (a ceiling for refinancing of supplier credits, C ceiling for buyer credits, B ceiling funds (see below)					
Funding							Provided by large institutional lenders	
Financing procedures & rates			Almost entirely supplier credit, about 1% lower interest rate than long-term credit market rate				PEFCO lends with Eximbank guarantees at market rates	
Special arrangements		Credits over 18 months with COFACE guarantee qualify for preferential financing under a special arrangement involving the Bank of France & BFCE	B ceiling financing by AKA			ECGD refinancing arrangement; refinance is extended by the government for amounts that are due to mature for payment more than 5 years after commencement of the credit period; the refinance rate		

				is fixed by the government & applies only to domestic currency loans; for that part of the credit that matures within 5 years & for credits from 2 to 5 years
Funding				
Central bank	Part of credit is rediscounted with Bank of France at 4.5% plus a commission	Rediscount facility with central bank at 2.1% above discount rate		
Other public bodies				
Capital markets	Commercial banks finance directly part of the credit at fixed market rates BFCE for maturities over 7 years	Funding by private banks at present a fixed revolving fund of DM 3 billion		
Other sources				
Financing procedures & rates	A blend of central bank refinancing & market rates results in credits at fixed consensus rates; maturities over 7 years are financed by BFCE at the blended rate		Only available for refinancing of supplier credits covering maximum 70% of contract value & repayable within 48 months; credits exceeding 2 years combined with private or ceiling A financing	Foreign currency lending at consensus rates, sterling being somewhat higher; all rates set by ECGD & fixed for life of credit
Interest subsidies (paid directly to exporter or lender)			Mediocredito Centrale pays interest rebates directly to banks and to foreign buyers when funds are not available for refinancing	For credits not financed directly by the government banks are entitled to a commercially based rate of return

Source: OECD.

TABLE 6.5
Effective cost of medium-term export credit
(as of June 1978)

	Percent per Annum		
	Typical Rate	Share of Contract Financed (%)	Cost of Funds to Borrower
Canada	N.A.	N.A.	N.A.
France	7.25a	61-74	8.10
Germany	8.00	0b	8.80
Italy	7.25	85	7.75
Japan	7.25a	70	7.85
U.K.	7.25	85	7.85
U.S.:			
CFF	7.75	42.5	9.05 (½ floating)
Discount	9.00	85	10.20 (fixed)
FICA/Bank Guar.c	9.64	0	10.34 (floating)

Source: Eximbank Report to Congress, January 1980.

N.A. = Not applicable.

[a]This is the blended rate resulting from combining official and private funds. The interest rate on the official portion is manipulated so that the blended rate is equal to the prevailing Arrangement minimum.

[b]Medium-term German export finance is usually provided by the private sector although supported by official credit insurance.

[c]Under the FICA and bank guarantee programs, all financing is done by private commercial banks; thus, the rate shown is the average prime rate for the period of this report plus 1.5%, which is a typical rate charged by the commercial banks under these programs.

      Eximbank has attempted to compete with the mixed credit arrangements offered by its competitors by reducing the interest rate it charges on its portion of the loan and by increasing its cover. Despite Eximbank's efforts, however, uncompetitive financing by the United States constitutes a significant obstacle to commercial expansion of technology sales to developing countries. An Eximbank review noted that 13 percent (7 of 55) of proposed Eximbank financed exports were lost from April 1978 to March 1979 due to uncompetitive financing. A recent GAO report detailing Eximbank's competitive posture suggesed that many firms simply do not formally apply to Eximbank because they do not expect to receive competitive financing, or in fact recognize they are unable to receive it.

Procedure

In addition to terms, formal and informal procedures that an official export financing organization follows are of particular interest to an exporter, and thus contribute to an effective export policy. Italy, Japan and the United Kingdom require the least documentation for export financing; even though credit insurance is often a prerequisite for financing in these countries, arranging for the insurance is a comparatively simple task. Further, once insurance has been approved, the financing is often a formality; in the United Kingdom, the insurance and financing functions are handled by a single agency. Most of the Europeans offer one-stop shopping--incorporating finance, guarantees, and marketing in one package. France and Germany require a bit more information about the proposed sale, but are still less demanding of information than the United States and Canada. As Eximbank notes, "An applicant requesting an Eximbank preliminary commitment (PC) for a direct loan must demonstrate the viability of the project, and financial information on the buyer must be provided."3 Further, in other industrial countries (particularly France and the United Kingdom), even before the application has been submitted, informal procedures have already given the exporter some idea as to the ultimate approval of the projects. In fact, in France, the Compagnie Francaise d'Assurance pour le Commerce Exterieur (COFACE), the official credit insurers, will provide an informal commitment to support even large and more complex projects within one week of an informal inquiry.

But it is not simply the nexus of other industrial policies that makes the United States uncompetitive in its official export financing. As noted in previous chapters, there are a number of obstacles that have been imposed on Eximbank.

Budgetary Limitations

Since Congress annually sets an authorization ceiling on Eximbank's direct lending, it limits the amount and number of credits that the Bank can provide. An individual financing package is made up of two components--the official and commercial--and the portion that Eximbank does not cover will have to be compensated for by a higher-priced commercial loan. Further, the Bank does not use direct loan authorization to finance medium-term loans or to finance exports under $5 million; additional authorization would be required to finance these activities. The first column of Table 6.6 (Budgetary Constraints) reveals that only Italy faces the limitations imposed by annual authorization ceilings--and even here, the situation is slowly changing. By having virtually unlimited authorization, other industrial countries are able to provide official support and provide for the lowest possible rates permitted by the Arrangement.

Unlike its competitors, Eximbank operates on a self-sustaining basis. But because the Bank must compete with other industrial country agencies that face no such constraint, it is not possible for the Bank to charge competitive interest rates and remain self-sustaining. Table 6.6 (Annual Appropriations) shows that only the United States and Canadian official credit agencies do not receive subsidies from general government revenues. During 1978, the Japanese and German export financing agencies borrowed from their governments at interest rates of 6.05 and 4.5 percent, respectively. Because inflation rates in France and in the United Kingdom were

98

TABLE 6.6
Government commitment to official export financing support

	Budgetary Constraints	Annual Appropriations
Canada	None	No
France	None	Yes
West Germany	None	--a
Italy	Substantial	Yes
Japan	Modest	--a
U.K.	None	Yes
U.S.	Substantial	No

Source: GAO Report to Congress, January 1980.

aThe low level of domestic interest rates has eliminated the need for appropriations to provide interest rate subsidies. The official credit insurers do have access to appropriations to cover annual losses but must remit to the government any profits earned in a particular year.

9.1 and 8.3 percent, borrowing at such low costs amounted to government subsidies to the export financing agencies, totaling $306 million and $210 million, respectively.

Foreign Components Restrictions

Many large-scale projects such as large infrastructure or manufacturing facilities involve the purchase of goods and services from a number of countries, including some--such as labor--from the importing country (local costs). Buyers attempt to arrange financing from the primary supplier for both local costs and for those items from other countries (foreign content financing). While the OECD Arrangement allows for local cost financing (up to the amount of cash payment, which is usually 15 percent of the export value) for poorer developing countries, the Arrangement makes no provision for relatively rich countres. German and Japanese export financing agencies support local costs up to the Arrangement maximum of 15 percent, while the French and British only finance local costs out of competitive pressure; U.S. Eximbank does not finance local costs. In fact, the United States has unsuccessfully attempted to change the Arrangement on local cost financing. Similarly, the United States does not finance foreign content financing. Japan will finance foreign content in Japanese exports if it is required by the buyer or if the goods are not available from Japan. While European countries finance up to 40 percent of the contract value for goods made in EEC countries and up to 10 percent from other countries, Eximbank has been only prepared to enter into cofinancing agreements with other suppliers--but only for the share of the export and only for the specific export.

Despite the Bank's best efforts, the United States suffers comparative disadvantage in a key policy instrument to promote technology exports
to developing countries. As in the case of uncompetitive interest rates, a
number of potential exporters simply do not approach the Bank for
financing, for fear that one of the obstacles will inhibit--or at least delay--
arranging terms. Political considerations, potential adverse domestic
impacts, uncertain Congressional authorization, and uncertain approval
have proved eminently frustrating to U.S. exporters.

Summary

European and Japanese governments are the largest customers and
business partners of many of their companies, and as such the companies
are the arms to national economic policies. In particular, the companies
are an integral part of a national export policy. As the governments seek
to develop preferred relationships with developing countries, liberal credit
terms are provided for company exports. The annual Eximbank survey of
bankers and exporters is reported in Table 6.7. This and other evidence
suggest that the credit terms available for U.S. exporters do not match
those available to European and Japanese competitors, and since now there
is often little difference in the technology, the contract usually goes to the
exporter with the best financial deal. Even if there are significant
technology differences, import decisions in developing countries are more
likely to be determined by economic and political considerations.

With these general points and comparisons in mind, let us look more
systematically at the export financing institutions and policies of the major
export competitors of the United States: France, Japan, the United
Kingdom and West Germany.

TABLE 6.7
U.S. exporter/banker rankings of official export credit facilities
(most competitive first, through least competitive last)

	Bankers			Exporters	
1979	1980	1981	1979	1980	1981[a]
France	France	France	Japan	Japan	France
Japan	Japan	U.K.	France	France	Japan
U.K.	Germany	Japan	U.K.	U.K.	U.K.
Germany	U.K.	Italy	Germany	Germany	Italy
U.S.	Italy	Germany	Italy	Italy	Germany
Italy	U.S.	Canada	U.S.	U.S.	Canada
		U.S.			U.S.

Source: U.S. Export-Import Bank, Report to the U.S. Congress on Export
Credit Competition, October 1981 and December 1982.

[a]Long-term programs.

FRANCE

France has been the most aggressive country in subsidizing export credits to improve its competitiveness. Table 6.8 illustrates this point by comparing French export credits to Middle Eastern countries with those of its four major export competitors. The region admittedly is not necessarily

TABLE 6.8
Export credits to Middle Eastern countries

Borrower	Lender				
	France	Japan	U.K.	U.S.	West Germany
Algeria					
1981	220,150	--	15,000	--	112,600
1980	296,663	--	--	7,500	269,043
1979	158,504	76,860	--	93,940	72,828
1978	26,411	215,155	--	533,005	122,295
1977	261,136	349,847	--	91,500	338,128
Tunisia					
1981	26,000	--	--	--	92,000
1980	42,689	--	--	7,525	--
1979	39,106	--	--	111,730	--
1978	133,705	--	--	--	--
1977	133,724	--	--	--	22,149
Egypt					
1981	89,000	--	244,000	--	57,800
1980	127,696	77,560	--	42,300	46,716
1979	210,688	27,818	32,171	91,375	26,976
1978	58,813	34,850	--	--	10,483
1977	99,652	32,831	--	--	--
Iran					
1979	--	--	--	--	1,891
1978	--	101,052	--	17,850	74,994
1977	--	258,176	--	--	--
Other Middle East					
1981	21,100	860	--	--	--
1980	26,212	40,000	70,419	276,335	--
1979	48,185	--	--	--	1,891
1978	25,657	7,397	--	--	120,844
1977	8,978	178,384	247,862	21,900	--

Source: OECD, Export Credits Group, Main Features of Officially Guaranteed Export Credit Transactions, 1977-1981.

representative of the universe of potential importers, but it is illustrative of the French approach to key countries, including those like Egypt for which previous colonial and economic ties are limited. The French have been able to dominate the European negotiating position within the OECD because nations of the European Community are represented as a bloc, requiring some concession to French interests. Export credits are granted in France on a virtual entitlement basis to any exporter. Credits are arranged and supplied by commercial banks, with the difference between their cost of funds and OECD Arrangement rates made up by the Treasury.

COFACE, the French foreign trade insurance company, administers the program and insures all export credits against default. The French invented mixed credits, that is, export credits mixed with development assistance, and have aggressively utilized this form of concessional financing, particularly in poorer countries and former colonies. The majority of French export credits are not mixed, however. Government policy on export credits is formulated in the Direction des Relations Economiques Exterieures (DREE) of the Ministry of External Affairs and Finance. COFACE operates under the supervision of DREE. The Banque Francaise du Commerce Exterieur (BFCE--the French foreign trade bank) also plays a role, in cooperation with the commercial banks.

Export credits are given for a period of up to two years (short-term credits), from two to seven years (medium-term credits) or for a period in excess of seven years (long-term credits). Separate procedures are required in each case. Short-term credits are financed at the base or "prime" lending rate, plus a 1 percent minimum bank charge and a COFACE premium if the credits are insured. The base rate was about 12 percent in early 1981, but it is adjusted frequently.[4]

Upon obtaining BFCE endorsement, medium-term export credits are rediscounted at preferential rates with the Bank of France. A "blending" rate between the preferential discount rate (5.5 percent in early 1981, including commission) and the base lending rate is determined by BFCE. This constitutes the refinancing rate for the exporter or the Bank. The higher the base rate, the greater the proportion to be refinanced by the Bank.[5] The cost of financing varies according to the maturity of the credit and the wealth of the importing country, in line with the OECD Arrangement.

Long-term export credits are financed entirely by the BFCE rather than the Bank of France. BFCE obtains its funding either from the capital markets or directly from the Treasury for this purpose.

Preferential refinancing of export credit requires an official guarantee or insurance from COFACE. Programs offered by COFACE include insurance against foreign exchange rate risks for exports payable in foreign currency, inflation and cost escalating insurance, individual policies covering commercial and political risks for light and heavy capital goods and large complexes, and nongovernmental insurance for exports of consumer goods, raw materials and equipment.

French export credit activity appears to be growing in recent years. New export loans increased 40 percent in 1981, with the financing directed principally in support of oil exploration and equipment, aircraft, shipbuilding, the automobile industry, turnkey manufacturing plants, farm products and public works. France's mixed credit program is the most effective element of its export financing activity. It enables French exporters to gain an initial competitive advantage that seems to lead to follow-on exports, in many cases at less subsidized rates. The program appears to be growing substantially; loans from the French Treasury for mixed credits have been increasing by nearly 30 percent per year.[6]

JAPAN

Official export credit financing is provided through the Export-Import Bank of Japan (EXIM), a government financial institution established in 1950. EXIM's capital stock was 937 billion yen in 1981, and it had a reserve of 50 billion yen. These figures are significant because they determine the total amount of outstanding credits granted by EXIM. Total credits cannot exceed the sum of its capital and reserves plus its maximum liability limit (equivalent to ten times its capital and reserves); thus, in 1981, total outstanding credits could not exceed approximately $55 billion, although the government can provide additional funds for capital increases. Although it cannot borrow from or rediscount with the Bank of Japan, EXIM may borrow from the Trust Fund Bureau, which handles savings through the government postal savings system at a fixed rate (7.5 percent in 1981) for a term of 10 years.

Much as other official export credit agencies, EXIM credits are blended with commercially available funds for financing medium- and long-term export contracts. The EXIM portion of the financing package is between 60 and 70 percent for capital goods exports and up to 55 percent for ship exports. While the government of Japan claims that the blended rate is in conformity with the OECD Arrangement, official Japanese export credit financing must be viewed as part of a comprehensive Japanese effort to promote exports. Thus Japan's EXIM enjoys vast financial resources and thus can offer export financing in far more cases at the floor of the Arrangement instead of only selected cases, as does its U.S. counterpart. Nor is it always the case that all officially supported Japanese exports are at the Arrangement's floor since Japan offers mixed aid and export credits for projects of "national importance" to developing countries. "Importance" in this case is somewhat vague, ranging from large projects in developing countries of substantial commercial value to Japan or support in exports to developing countries that will help Japan ensure access to raw materials (such as petroleum) or to large markets.

Perhaps the most effective component of Japan's export support is the close cooperation between public and private sectors--and the great flexibility such cooperation can provide. While there has been substantial publicity on the support the Japanese government has provided to manufacturers of cars and consumer electronics in their exports to developed countries, including the United States, an example of Japanese contacts with Mexico beginning in the late 1970s is a less-known but telling case of how official export credit financing fits into overall Japanese international economic policy. Concerned about ensuring its supplies of oil, Japan acted to strengthen its commercial relations with a number of oil exporters including Mexico. Beginning with the August 1979 oil agreement between then-President Lopez Portillo, former Foreign Minister Sunao Sonoda and MITI Minister Masumi Esaki in which Mexico pledged to export 100,000 barrels per day to Japan, Japan aimed to broaden "economic interchanges between Mexico and Japan . . . with the oil deal as a starting point." In return for Mexico's offer of crude oil, the Japanese government decided to extend $500 million in financing of Pemex's petroleum-related facilities, with Japanese Export-Import Bank covering 70 percent of the financing. Japanese and Mexican officials met to discuss technical cooperation in several areas including the construction of a steel-making complex at Las Truchas, the establishment of two seaside industrial zones, development of petrochemical, fertilizer and electrical machinery industries, and the construction of tourist resorts.

By January 1980, the Japanese government had already organized the details for the Las Truchas complex. The Japanese Federation of Economic Organizations, MITI, and three main private steelmakers arranged the financing of some $600 billion yen through the Japanese Export-Import Bank; further, private Japanese interests such as Nippon Steel Corporation, and the government through its Overseas Economic Cooperation Fund (OECF) agreed to set up a joint "Mexico Steel Works Corporation Company." At the same time, the Japan Federation of Economic Organization organized a setup for Japan's cooperation in Mexico's other industrial projects, such as harbor construction, if requested by the Mexican government. Responding to the Mexican government's desire that Mexican oil exports be part of a "broad scheme of cooperation" in industrial development, Japan developed plans for a $1 billion steel project in preparation for Prime Minister Ohira's visit in May 1980. The project involved loans from the Japanese Export-Import Bank, grants from OECF, and aid; this proposal played a key role in successful negotiations for long-term oil supplies.

A similar mixing of commercial and aid policies and public- and private-sector cooperation has characterized subsequent Japanese-Mexican relations. Further, while mixed credits had been granted on energy projects under which Japan would import most of the energy sources produced, EXIM has relaxed conditions for loans on resource development. In August 1983, EXIM signed a contract with Mitsui Oil Exploration Co. to provide them with a low-interest loan for natural gas development off Thailand where the two companies plan to sell most of the gas discovered.

UNITED KINGDOM

The United Kingdom has an export credit program rather similar to the French system. It is administered by the Export Credits Guarantee Department of the Trade Ministry with commercial banks as the suppliers of funds. Credits are on an entitlement basis, at OECD Arrangement minimum rates, with an interest subsidy provided to the banks, and guarantees through ECGD. The United Kingdom has not been adamant about keeping interest rate guidelines in the OECD relatively low to allow latitude for subsidization, but it routinely offers these subsidies. The United Kingdom has pioneered several forms of insurance coverage, also adopted by France and others, such as foreign currency (exchange rate guarantees and cost escalation insurance). Mixed credits are used on occasion.

For fixed rate lending in support of exports, commercial banks are guaranteed a commercial rate of return by the government. About 5 percent of total U.K. exports are handled on this basis; all have maturities in excess of two years. The government established an export credit support facility in 1980, allocating about 5 percent of the foreign assistance budget to attempt to match the mixed export credit practices of its competitors. With few exceptions (such as shipbuilding), interest support by the government is not available for exports to members of the European Community.

All U.K. banks judged acceptable under the 1979 Banking Act can act as sole lenders or syndicate leaders in an export financing project. Interest rate support from public funds is not constrained by annual ceilings, but they are, of course, limited by overall controls on public expenditure. In 1980 (the last year for which figures are available), public expenditure in support of fixed rate export credits totaled £357 million.[7]

ECGD risk insurance or guarantee covering nonpayment is required for public-funded export financing. The department's activities are ultimately subject to the consent of the Treasury, but little day-to-day supervision is, in fact, maintained. The ECGD must reject risky ventures in its credit insurance decision, however, because it is required to insure without net cost to public funds.

ECGD's authority is divided into commercial and national interest accounts. Commercial accounts are insured on a purely commercial basis and constitute nearly 90 percent of its insurance activity. The remaining "national interest accounts" are transactions that do not meet normal commercial standards and resemble those treated under the U.S. Eximbank's Export Expansion Facility. ECGD has been under some pressure to reduce its expenditures recently; premium rates have been increased in response to a 50 percent rise in claims in 1980-1981.[8]

Following the French example, the British inaugerated a mixed credits program in January 1981. Government statements emphasized reluctance in taking this decision, however, and favored international efforts to ban this kind of trade distortion. The apparent strategy was to match competitor programs to remove the underlying incentives. OECD efforts to reduce these distortions met with little progress, however, largely due to French intrasigence. Negotiations have continued well into 1983 with periodic transatlantic trade war threats and British conflict with France and Greece within the European Community.

WEST GERMANY

Official report credits are provided by two institutions, the government-owned Kreditanstalt fur Wiederaubau (KfW), with two government-supported promotion funds, and AKA, a private sector organization that has access for parts of its export financing to a rediscounting facility of the central bank.

Although KfW was established in 1948 to finance postwar reconstruction, since 1955 KfW has played a key role in directly supporting long-term German exports; and since the early 1960s, KfW has been the official agency for the German capital aid program for developing countries. In keeping with KfW's broad objectives, the organization is managed by a 30-member board of directors that includes 6 federal ministers, 5 members of the Bundesrat, representatives from the Bundesbank, and 16 members from different sectors of the economy.

KfW's export credit financing is supported by two government funds: Fund I, a revolving credit of DM 500 million; and Fund II, a yearly allocation of DM 90 million from the government, which is reimbursed to the government as the loans are amortized. These funds are lent to KfW at 4.5 percent, and KfW combines them in a 1:3 ratio with funds raised on the capital markets. According to German government figures, with an average of DM 200 in special funds available each year, KfW can provide about DM 800 million in long-term export credits annually. Although some credit has been extended on sales of airbuses and other items to developed countries, Funds I and II are primarily used to support German exports to developing countries. To qualify for support, the transaction must be officially insured or guaranteed; the term of the loan under Funds I and II must be at least seven years (although the restriction does not apply to medium-sized exporters with sales of less than DM 200 million). As with other official export credit entities with limited resources, KfW blends its subsidized funds with those from the capital markets; only in transactions less than DM 25 million does KfW fully finance the credit element from Funds I and II; for contracts between DM 25 and DM 50 million, the Funds may not provide more than DM 22.5 million; for contracts over DM 50 million, Funds I and II provide proportionately less support as the contract values increase up to a maximum of DM 85 million, even if the contract value exceeds DM 200 million. Table 6.9 provides an example as of March 1981 of blended KfW and market rates.

Set up in 1951, AKA is a private syndicate composed of 56 commercial banks. Exports are supported by three loan windows, Lines A, B, and C; funds for Lines A and C are drawn from member banks. Funds for Line B credits are obtained through a rediscounting facility at the Bundesbank at a preferential rate of 1.5 percent above its discount rate.

Under Line A, which has a ceiling of DM 10 billion, application is made by a supplier through a member bank for refinancing supplier credits. There is no government intervention in Line A financing. AKA typically refinances 70 to 75 percent of the contract value (15 to 20 percent cash payment). Maximum credit length is seldom more than ten years.

Under Line B, which has DM 5 billion available, AKA provides supplier credits to developing countries with a 1- to 4-year term. As noted above, the interest rate charged is 1.5 percent above the official Bundesbank discount rate, with an additional 0.6 percent bill of exchange tax and an 0.1 percent commitment fee charged yearly. Up to 70 percent of the contract value can be financed from the B line, with the remainder combined in the credit from the A line so that the exporter can receive full financing with terms exceeding four years. Since the A line portion carries market rates and the B line is subsidized, the blended rate is often far below market rates, although the portion of subsidized finance decreases over time; all payments made by the buyer are first used to pay off the B line credit so the proportion not covered by the B line gradually increases.

Under Line C, member banks provide buyer credits with terms of two to ten years at floating or fixed market rates, with no government subsidies. Although the C line was once hardly used because German exporters preferred to arrange their own supplier exports, since the mid-1970s, there has been stronger demand for buyer credit financing.

TABLE 6.9
Synopsis of West German interest rates as of March 1981;
examples of average financing costs, using all types of
preferential financing to the maximum possible extent (percent)

Length of Credit	3 years	8 years		10 years	
Source of Finance	AKA+M Suppl. Cr.	AKA+M Suppl. Cr.	KfW+AKA Buyer's Cr.	AKA+M Suppl. Cr.	KfW+M Buyer's Cr.
Market rate (1) (fixed/ floating)	11.5/ 13.5	11.5/ 13.5	11.5/ 13.5	11.5/ 13.5	11.5/ 13.5
AKA (floating) (2)	10.5	13.1	13.5	13.25	13.5
KfW (fixed)	-	-	9.5	-	9.5
Average rate of interest (floating)(3)	11.0	13.25	11.5	13.5	11.5
Bank charges (4)/(5)	0.3	0.1	0.1	0.1	0.1
Insurance premium (6)/(4)	0.7	0.6	0.6	0.55	0.55
Average financing costs per year (floating)(7)	12.0	14.0	12.2	14.2	12.2

Source: OECD, The Export Financing Systems in OECD Member Countries, pp. 115-116.

(1) Fixed rate: estimate based on capital market conditions, currently not normally available for export credits; floating rate: AKA rates for Lines A and C.

(2) Line B combined with Line A.

(3) To the nearest one-quarter percent.

(4) Converted to annual basis.

(5) Total estimated at 1 percent of amount of loan (payable once only).

(6) For public-sector buyers; twice as high for private buyers.

(7) First year only (average of an 8.5 percent per annum market rate on 20 percent of the total volume, 7.25 percent per annum on a Line A credit for 40 percent and 5.6 percent on a Line B credit).

NOTES

1.   There is considerable disagreement among U.S. authorities on developing country evaluations of comparative export credits under a floating exchange rate regime.   The General Accounting Office (GAO) claims that because of the difficulty associated with attempting to predict exchange rate trends, most developing countries employ the nominal rates. Treasury disagrees, claiming that nominal interest rate illusion does not exist in fact or in theory.   According to Treasury officials, buyers ordinarily do have some exchange rate expectations in mind when considering competing export credit offers; some buyers may suffer from interest rate illusion, but it is unlikely that all buyers are ignorant to the difference between dollar finance and Swiss franc finance.   Treasury concludes, "It makes little sense to recommend that the U.S. government should answer an illusion of this type by offering, say, the Swiss franc interest rate for a U.S. dollar credit." See the letter from C. Fred Bergsten to J. K. Fasick, Director, International Divison, GAO, February 4, 1980.

2.   Under the Italian and U.K. system, the Arrangement minimum extends only to dollar denominated financing; on domestic currency credits, the rates are somewhat higher.

3.   Eximbank Report to Congress, January 1980, p. 22.

4.   OECD, The Export Financing Systems in OECD Member Countries (Paris: OECD, 1982), p. 98.

5.   Ibid., p. 97.

6.   U.S. Export-Import Bank, Report to the U.S. Congress on Export Credit Competition, December 1982, p. 48.

7.   OECD, Export Credit Financing Systems in OECD Member Countries (Paris: OECD, 1982), p. 237.

8.   U.S. Export-Import Bank, Report to the U.S. Congress on Export Credit Competition, December 1982, p. 69.

7
Alternative Criteria

Throughout most of its history, Eximbank has not had a prominent role in U.S. trade policy. The Bank existed as an independent institution, under relatively little scrutiny from Congress or policy coordination with other executive branch agencies. Many Congressmen knew little about the Bank other than that it supported exports and returned a dividend to the Treasury each year. The long-term and low interest rates the Bank offered were synonymous with the strength of U.S. capital markets, as were the goods it financed with the leadership of U.S. industry. The Bank was passive in its allocation of resources, supporting requests that were presented to it with the appropriate programs, based on the type of export and considerations of credit-worthinesss. Eximbank loan officers enjoyed access to a broad range of resources with which to structure financings; resources were seldom constraining, and the Bank frequently introduced new programs where they could be useful in supporting exports. In this environment the Bank's policy was straightforward and clear: to support exports requiring financing while seeking reasonable reassurance of repayment. Policy planning was of little concern; the Bank had no formal policy analysis office until recently.

In the current environment, the need for careful policy planning is paramount. The Bank is torn by the need to be competitive, and yet fiscally responsible, within the framework of declining resources relative to the potential demand for its loans. The concern of exporters is evident in the strong lobbying over the proposed budget levels for the Bank, and the formation of a lobby group aimed specifically at a stronger Eximbank, the Coalition for Employment through Exports. On the other hand, OMB has supported a market-related interest rate for the Bank, and insists it must get by on reduced resources along with other federal programs. If one assumes a continuation of the resource constraints on the Bank, and its unwillingness to sustain large losses indefinitely, the flexibility of the Bank in terms of alternative criteria is limited. If one assumes also that the Arrangement negotiations will be frustrated in completely eliminating export credit subsidies, the Bank will continue to operate in an environment of intense competition. The current policy has been based implicitly on riding out the short term until progress is made in the negotiations, U.S. interest rate levels decline, and economic activity accelerates. While these developments would take some of the pressure off the Bank, they still would not solve the need for deliberate policy planning. This chapter poses several alternatives for the Bank in the current environment, and examines future trends that affect export credits and Eximbank policies. As a means of deliberate policy planning, the most immediate step the Bank can take is the specification and implementation of explicit lending criteria.

EXPLICIT CRITERIA FOR DIRECT CREDIT SUPPORT

Explicit targeting criteria represent in many ways a more controversial lending policy than targeting by case assessment. Currently, the Bank maintains it can meet the needs of exporters in the most important cases with its available resources. In doing so it does not outwardly deny direct credit support to an identifiable group, and in essence finesses the issue of allocation under reduced resources. While it may be a safer approach in this respect, reliance on individual case assessment may reduce the Bank's credibility in the long run because of the weight it places on board decisions and the inconsistent response across cases.

The adherence to explicit criteria in determining the need for Eximbank support would formalize and rationalize the targeting of resources. Targeting based on specific, explicit criteria, whether by a more systematic extension of existing criteria or by industry, would give a focus to the Bank's lending program. It would reduce the influence of individual assessments on cases, promote consistency, and provide clear guidelines for the staff in responding to cases. It would represent a reasoned, deliberate policy response to the limitations placed on the Bank's resources. It would send a clear signal to the export sector of the support the firms can receive from the Bank, and of the rationale behind that support. The adherence to explicit criteria would also reduce the vulnerability of the board to political pressure or exporter lobbying. Board decisions that have the appearance of succumbing to outside influence, such as the Ansett loan case, damage the Bank's credibility whether the allegations of influence are valid or not. The use of explicit criteria would enable the Bank to publicly justify its decisions without this stigma. The Bank's credibility is also an important factor in its ability to command resources in the Congressional budget allocation process. The presentation of explicit criteria for a direct credit support would improve the Bank's accountability before Congress, through delineating in a precise manner what its programs can accomplish.

The most immediate basis for specifying a set of criteria is the formalization and extension of existing decisionmaking guidelines. This formulation would place the emphasis on determining the characteristics of products and buyers that make financing more important at the policy planning level at the Bank, rather than on an individual case level. The Bank has done this with aircraft, by specifying which airplanes will be eligible for direct credit support, and imposing a maximum cover of 42.5 percent.[1] The "monopoly position" criterion is also explicit. The financing sensitivity of buyers is also defined to an extent by the presumption that the Bank will not normally finance sales to rich countries. The use of explicit criteria would not necessarily redirect the Bank's lending policies, but would formalize and rationalize the decisionmaking process.

There are several criteria that could be employed at the Bank that are consistent with current policy. For example, the Bank could require submission of bid solicitations in order to document the existence of foreign competition. This would effectively mean that the Bank would only support exports in international tender situations, and would eliminate the negotiated sales to single U.S. suppliers the Bank still occasionally finances. Doing so would formalize the Bank's role in meeting foreign competition. Similarly, the Bank could formalize its reluctance to finance sales to other industrial countries by excluding them from eligibility for direct credit support. Doing so would release Bank resources for support of exports to countries where financing is a much more important consideration. For example, the Bank authorized over $1 billion in loans to Canada alone in FY 1981. Consistent with the Bank's findings that private-sector buyers are less sensitive to financing in their choice among suppliers, the Bank could implement this as a criterion by financing only sales to public-sector entities.

These criteria are all restrictive in nature, but in a manner consistent with the Bank's current targeting of resources. These examples are intended to be illustrative of ways the Bank could respond to the need to target resources effectively by specifying explicit criteria for direct credit support. Denial of direct credit support on this basis would not be a complete withdrawal of support from those cases, but a denial of subsidized support. Guarantees and the assistance of the Bank in arranging commercial financing would still be important means of support.

The use of more explicit criteria in this manner would reduce the role of outside influences on individual credit decisions. The determination of whether a case met Eximbank criteria would be much simpler than in the current assessment process. Adherence to specific criteria would reduce the Bank's flexibility to respond to conditions of particular cases, for example, to meet particularly concessional terms offered in mixed credits, or the granting of Eximbank loans to further foreign policy or other trade policy goals. However, this loss of flexibility, if it actually does prove to be a drawback, must be offset against the progress that would be made toward the formation and implementation of a consistent, well-defined export credit program. A decrease in flexibility on individual cases would also mean a reduction in the ability of other federal agencies to influence board decisions. However, their influence would be maintained in the formation of Bank policy and lending criteria. The specification of lending criteria would preempt individual case assessments as the primary determinant of eligibility, and hence would redirect the influence of other agencies, as well as industry, to the formation of policy at the Bank. In addition to the benefits associated with greater consistency and accountability mentioned above, the emphasis on policy formation over case decisions would, therefore, help to improve the responsiveness of the Bank to new policy initiatives.

TARGETING BY INDUSTRY

Targeting to specific industries represents an alternative means of allocating Eximbank resources that would also be explicit and predictable in their application. The Bank has avoided explicitly designating industries for support, preferring to maintain a passive approach that relies on the importance of financing in each case. However, the resulting pattern of support across industries is highly concentrated, as was discussed in

Chapter 3. Thus, targeting by industry need not entail a radical redirection of resources in the direct loan program. Selecting the basis upon which to assess industries for eligibility for direct credit is not a clear-cut matter, and several approaches could be taken.

The Bank currently employs several industry-related criteria, both explicitly and implicitly. The financing of projects as opposed to products results in a general classification by industry that supports large project exports. As a result of this criterion, Eximbank has become the primary source of export finance for the aircraft, electric power (especially nuclear) and certain manufacturing plants such as steel, cement, and chemicals. Competition from other capital goods exporters has also led to the dependence of these industries on official export credits. The Bank also monitors industries to determine their need for export credits, as part of its targeting efforts. The characteristics the Bank assesses include the competitive position of U.S. firms, the active use of subsidized credit by foreign competitors, and dependence on export markets, particularly in developing countries. This informal monitoring has proved to be a means of nominating industries for direct credit support, but has not constituted a viable basis for screening out industries less dependent on export credits. In order to target resources on an industry basis, some further means of classifying industries is needed.

The Bank has attempted a more stringent application of an industry-based selection criterion in the offshore oil field equipment industry. As was described in Chapter 2, the determination was made that denial of direct credit support would not affect the overall health of the industry because of its high-order backlogs, strong competitive position and lack of high dependence on export markets. This determination was supported by the Bank's "Follow-up Studies on PC Dispositions," which showed a lack of sensitivity to the denial of Eximbank financing in the industry.[2] The decision was made, however, with the knowledge that it would mean some export sales lost, but that these would not have a great effect on the survival or competitiveness of the industry. Industry targeting on a basis such as this would provide a means of directing Bank resources, and could be applied in a systematic manner.

The rationale used in the oilfield equipment case is suggestive of an alternative approach to industry targeting based on considerations of industrial policy. In general, the United States has refrained from an activist industrial policy that singles out "winners" for government support. However, the Bank is confronted with a need to target its resources effectively, and at a minimum could identify those industries that are unlikely to remain competitive even with subsidized export credits, and direct its loans to other sectors. There are several indicators that are useful in such a determination: a declining market share (domestic and export), a lack of revealed comparative advantage, the exit of firms from the industry, a dropoff in new investment, the lack of technological advance and innovation by U.S. firms, and the emergence of lower-cost competitors. The effect of denying direct credit support to weak industries would be to speed up the adjustment process over what it would have been if the Bank had offset foreign subsidies with direct loans, and to reallocate resources to those sectors that could extend their comparative advantage beyond a 'normal' (without Eximbank support) time period.

However, the targeting of loans to strong U.S. industries, with the rationale of encouraging their growth and preempting the emergence of competitors, may be superfluous. If U.S. firms have a distinct competitive advantage, export credits will not be a crucial factor in promoting the growth of the industry. Export credits are an effective tool for promoting an industry where there is competition with subsidized credit or a lack of access to finance for the importer. If the use of export credits were expanded by the United States to cover leading industries such as computers, this would only require that potential competitors also support their industries with subsidized credit, leading to an increase in the competitive use of export credits. In the face of determined efforts by other nations to develop industries to compete with the United States, the aggressive use of export credits is unlikely to be a persuasive deterrent.

The most effective means of targeting by industry would be to expand upon the criteria the Bank currently employs and incorporate considerations of long-term viability and competitiveness. Within the framework of capital goods industries, which are faced with competition in subsidized credit and dependent on export markets, a form of triage assessment would be made. This would involve identifying those industries that would remain competitive even without Eximbank support, those that would be disadvantaged by a lack of support, and those that would contract or cease to be competitive in export markets even with Eximbank support. Direct credits would then be concentrated on the second group of industries. With respect to the first group, this triage policy would be a formalization of the criteria the Bank has applied with respect to the oilfield industry and in its denial of direct credit support in cases where the U.S. producer has a significant technological advantage. In the third group of declining industries, adoption of this type of policy would represent a clear departure for the Bank. However, the effect on U.S. industry will be small if these industries are unable to stay competitive for more fundamental reasons than export financing. Even if U.S. policy called for some means of supporting a declining industry, export credits would not be as effective as measures aimed directly at the causes of decline, or more positive adjustment policies such as retraining.

The implementation of any policy that targets loans by industry will prove problematic given the resistance from those industries left out. In the recent case involving the oilfield equipment industry, the pressure on the Bank for singling out a particular industry was immediate and intense, and contributed to the reversal of that policy. The reaction from industries singled out for demise is likely to be even stronger. The ability of the Bank to withstand the resulting political pressure will be the main determinant of the successful implementation of an industry targeting approach. The Bank's position in this regard would be stronger if it were applied in an orchestrated manner based on the need for a triage approach, than it has been in the isolated applications of industry specific policies.

OPTIONS ON RATES AND TERMS

The interest rate, fees, percentage of cover and maturity the Bank offers do not constitute selection criteria for direct credit support, but taken together they form the basis of the Bank's competitive posture. In the current environment of subsidized export credit competition, the Bank's choices on interest rate policy are a direct function of its willingness and ability to sustain losses in order to achieve greater competitiveness. If the Bank is to be competitive with subsidized rates in the cases it does support, an interest rate involving some degree of subsidy is probably required. The problem lies in the determination of a competitive rate. It is clearly desirable to reduce the subsidy in interest rates to the lowest degree possible while maintaining competitiveness. One means would be to offer the same degree of subsidy, or discount from market rates, as competitors who subsidize rates on an average basis. This would act to ensure competitiveness, perhaps to a degree that is unnecessary in terms of removing the distortion of foreign subsidies. Implicit in the Bank's current approach is the attempt to raise rates until the point where the threshold of competitiveness is reached. This may involve some trial and error, but it is a point that should be established. From the perspective of the need to target direct loan resources selectively, a relatively higher interest rate is desirable because it reduces the differential between a direct loan and a financial guarantee.

The alternative of keeping interest rates within a known range of competitiveness with Arrangement rates may require continuing losses. To date there has been no consensus on whether the economic benefits of a highly subsidized, fully competitive export credit program justify the use of government resources. This question has been addressed only in terms of whether the Bank should sustain losses, which disguises the issue of whether the federal government should devote resources to subsidized export credits. This question would be made explicit if appropriations are required to cover the Bank's losses. This is perhaps the best reason for subsidizing large, negative spreads through a separate appropriation, if they are necessary for competitiveness, rather than running down the Bank's capital and reserves. If the Bank can only be competitive at interest rates below its cost of funds, then some version of the "war chest" is the best means of directing resources to this use. It puts the issue in the proper context of budgetary allocation, rather than keeping it an internal matter of Bank policy. It would also force Congress to deal directly with the problem of providing competitive finance and give some guidance to the Bank as to what U.S. export credit policy should be.

The problems inherent in the reorientation of Bank policy on losses are illustrated in the 2 percent commitment fee. The fee was intended to offset the losses due to loans made in the previous administration. This is placing an additional burden on current loans that is related to past policies on competitiveness. If the policy of the Bank is to operate at a profit, then this should relate to its interest rate and cost of funds to maintain profitability over the long run. The preoccupation with short-run results places an extra constraint on the Bank's current competitiveness beyond what would otherwise be required for profitability.

The percentage of cover the Bank assumes is a means of controlling the term of private participation and lowering the blended rate to the borrower. However, the term of participation finance is not the main determinant of the importance of the percentage the Bank assumes. If this were the case the Bank could reduce its standard cover below 42.5 percent, especially on loans under 10 years, while still keeping the participation period in a standard medium-term range for commercial bank loans of 3-5 years. The main reason for increasing the cover is to lower the blended rate. This is done at the cost of utilizing more direct loan resources for a single case. Hence, there is a direct trade-off between greater competitiveness in a single case, and the ability to support more cases with direct credits which extends the breadth of competitiveness. The alternatives must be weighed on this basis. If the demand for direct loans is relatively great, then cover should be standardized at a lower percentage in order to extend the Bank's resources over as many cases as possible.

The extension of maturity has been the major instrument of increasing competitiveness used by the Bank. These extensions were made selectively, and have been used primarily to counter grandfather loans and especially concessional credits. With the recent revisions in the OECD Arrangement, the United States is bound not to extend maturities beyond the agreed terms. Thus as long as the other members keep to the agreement on rates and terms, the extension of maturities will not be available as a means of increasing competitiveness. The strategy of derogation from Arrangement terms on maturity was a relatively easy step for the Bank to take. Unlike interest rate subsidization, it does not affect the current income of the Bank. It also does not utilize additional program resources as does the extension of cover. The ease of funding longer maturities in the U.S. government bond market, compared to the shorter terms available in most European capital markets, made the extension of maturities an effective means of increasing competitiveness and pressuring other countries to revise the Arrangement. In the event of a breakdown in discipline in the Arrangement, derogation on maturity probably will be used again as a means of improving competitiveness.

The parameters of interest rate, commitment fee, cover and maturity all determine the relative competitiveness of an Eximbank direct loan. They also determine the level of subsidy in the loan. Any measure to increase competitiveness also increases the subsidy. The preference of the Bank for the extension of maturity stems from the fact that it subsidizes in a relatively invisible manner. If one assumes the restriction that the Bank remain profitable and be limited in budget authority, extension of maturity is the only real tool for increasing competitiveness. However, this is limited if the United States is to stay within the current terms of the Arrangement. If the Bank must subsidize interest rates to remain competitive, this should be done through an appropriation for that purpose, with the magnitude of the subsidy determined as part of the budgetary process, not as part of internal Eximbank policy.

INCREASING PRIVATE-SECTOR PARTICIPATION IN EXPORT CREDITS

The role that private-sector financial institutions can serve in financing exports is limited by the level of subsidization in official export credits. In order to compete effectively against foreign subsidized credit, some element of subsidy is probably required. With continued progress in the Arrangement in reducing subsidies, and with a decline in market interest rates in the United States, there will be opportunities for a greater involvement of commercial banks in export finance. Capitalization of these opportunities is important for several reasons. An increase in commercial bank participation would help to extend the resources of Eximbank. Major international banks have access to funding in other currency markets, and can thus facilitate export finance in low interest rate currencies in cases where buyers prefer those currencies. In general, commercial banks have been innovative and responsive in developing new financing methods and instruments, and a stronger role for them in export finance would encourage continued innovation. The export credit function in most major banks has become a kind of brokerage service among different nations' official export credit services, advising multinationals on the financing implications of sourcing decisions. While this is a natural activity for international banks whose major clients include multinational corporations and foreign governments, some means of increasing the attractiveness for these banks of financing U.S. exports may be desirable.

One means of fostering a greater role for commercial banks would be to develop a refinancing facility for export credits along the lines of the discount loan program. This would allow commercial banks to take a more active role in terms of managing and structuring loans. A refinancing window would be more attractive for banks because they could collect a fee and get the loan off their books. Commercial banks in general have preferred this type of export credit system, which is the basis of most European systems, because it allows them a greater role than participating in direct credits and ultimately is more profitable for them. Implementation of this type of program would require the specification of explicit criteria for eligibility, and the Bank could retain control over the types of credits financed in a manner consistent with explicit criteria for the direct loan program. This type of program could be initiated experimentally for certain types of exports, or in specific industries. The most immediate means would be to expand from the medium-term sector where commercial banks have been the primary actors. This could be accomplished within the current institutional framework by enlarging the discount loan program to include larger transactions and longer maturities, in essence turning over the lower range of direct credits to commercial banks. If export trading companies prove to be viable instruments of international trade association, the window could be directed at them. At present, the proposed export trading company legislation stipulates only the provision of Eximbank guarantees. The availability of a refinancing facility would also serve to encourage the development of export trading companies.

A related area where Eximbank could be more responsive to the role of commercial banks is increased flexibility in its guarantee program. At the present time Eximbank offers financial guarantees that cover commercial and political risk. In some cases of sales to private buyers, however, a commercial risk guarantee may have little attractiveness for a commercial bank. They often prefer to accept the commercial risk in return for a higher spread, while still desiring a political risk guarantee. In a similar manner, Eximbank has never clearly stated any policy on leasing transactions. Leasing is an increasingly important means of financing capital goods exports, in which commercial banks often assume the intermediary role. To meet the needs of banks in these types of cases, the Eximbank could be more flexible in the structuring of its guarantees and the development of policies to cover transactions such as leasing.

Another means of transferring export finance back to the private sector is illustrated in the efforts of U.S. aircraft manufacturers to develop new instruments for the financing of aircraft exports. The instrument being discussed is the international equipment trust certificate, which would be structured in a similar manner as equipment trust certificates (with a government guarantee) that are used extensively to finance domestic sales of capital goods such as aircraft. The chief advantage of this type of financing mechanism is that it allows longer maturities at interest rates lower than market rates available either directly from banks or the bond markets because of the tax advantages to the lender. The international equipment trust certificate would be aimed at both the sales of Airbus and competing U.S. aircraft, in order to end the competition in subsidized credit and extend the maturity to reflect the useful life and payback period of aircraft. However, in the event of failure of agreement by Airbus partners, such a mechanism could be instituted unilaterally by the United States if it proved attractive to purchasers. Efforts such as these can become an important means of utilizing the strength of U.S. capital markets to increase private-sector participation in export finance.

THE FUTURE ENVIRONMENT FOR EXPORT CREDITS

The foregoing discussion of alternative criteria for Eximbank focused on the current environment for export credits. However, several trends in the world economy are likely to have an impact on export credit issues and questions of policy facing Eximbank. One of the principal forces behind the competition in subsidized export credits of the past few years has been the stagnation in most of the industrial countries. Subsidized export credits were seen as a means of maintaining employment in capital goods industries, which faced declining domestic markets due to the recession. While the outlook for the industrial economies through the mid-1980s is still uncertain, a rapid resumption of sustained economic growth is unlikely. Continued stagnation or a slow recovery will mean a continued emphasis on export credits--as well as other forms of subsidy--as a means of maintaining employment.

Aggravating the general economic situation in the industrial countries are the trade adjustment problems created by changing patterns of comparative advantage in manufactured goods. Increased competition from low cost and high productivity countries has increased the demand for protective measures from industry to delay or offset the impact of import penetration. While the impact of these imports is primarily in basic industries, the resulting effect on overall employment levels also creates pressure for means of stimulating other industries. The competitive challenge from the NICs will increase over the coming decade, which will compound the problem of slow economic growth and trade adjustment. The expansion of industrial capacity in the NICs will also create a continuing market for capital goods, and the focus of competition among capital goods exporters will increasingly be the developing countries. Thus, as the industrial countries continue the shift away from basic manufacturing sectors into services and more sophisticated industries including capital goods, export credits will become increasingly important.

The reliance on a directed industrial policy by European countries and Japan in this environment suggests that export credits, along with other protectionist and distorting measures, will continue to be important tools for implementing industrial policy. The problems of stagnation and trade adjustment have created or intensified trade disputes among the industrial countries to the point where overall relations among the Western powers have deteriorated drastically. In this context of trade disputes in automobiles, steel, agriculture, and East-West trade, international agreements on the control of government intervention in trade will be increasingly difficult to achieve. Recent GATT Ministerial talks have been jeopardized by the inability to resolve outstanding trade disputes. Indeed, in the current environment it is somewhat remarkable that the OECD nations were able to reach a new agreement on export credits. However, without a resolution of existing trade tensions, it is increasingly unlikely that continued progress in reducing the latitude for subsidization in export credits can be achieved. At the very least, the linkage with other trade issues may compromise U.S. negotiating efforts within the OECD. It was suggested in the previous chapter that the Subsidies Code may be a more effective forum for the international control of export credits; this may become an even more important aspect of U.S. trade policy if the inability to reach new agreements forces the reliance on existing mechanisms of control. Even though the same resistance can be expected as in the OECD, it may be worth a try. One of the reasons cited there for treatment of export credits in the Subsidies Code was the emergence of the NICs as capital goods exporters, and the need to incorporate them into international agreements.

The increasing role of the NICs as capital goods exporters poses several problems for U.S. trade policy. In most cases where they have developed capital goods industries capable of competing internationally, this has been facilitated by activist government policies of support and promotion. This support extends to export credits, without even the moderating influence of the terms of the OECD Arrangement. The impact of the NICs will be concentrated in the equipment for basic industries in which they have an extensive base such as steel, cement, and transportation equipment. Competition in these sectors will mean an increasing demand for Eximbank support for U.S. firms in these industries. Offsetting these subsidies would entail a redirection of Eximbank lending to plant exports for these basic industries. In addition, the NICs may utilize other means of capturing markets in developing countries which are already evident in the pattern of South-South trade. Chief among these is a willingness to negotiate barter and countertrade deals. In addition, a preference by developing countries for increased South-South trade is emerging in forums such as UNCTAD. This factor may be even stronger because of the transfer of technology inherent in capital goods exports: developing countries may prefer to import technology developed or adapted in other developing countries. Again, these developments will place an added burden on Eximbank to offset the support enjoyed by the NIC exporters.

The ability to include the NICs in agreements limiting export credits will be related to broader efforts to graduate these countries out of preferential trade agreements and into full compliance with the GATT and other multilateral accords. The United States is currently initiating proposals for a new round of trade negotiations with the developing countries. In this context, the control of subsidized export credits will be an additional objective to be offset against greater market access for developing country exports. However, it is within this type of forum with reciprocal benefits from graduation and closer compliance with existing trade agreements that the inclusion of the NICs in export credit agreements is most likely to be effected. Their accession to the OECD Arrangement is less likely because of their lack of negotiating leverage and reciprocal benefits. The importance of incorporating the NICs into an agreement on export credits will increase in the future as they become increasingly sophisticated and competitive in the production of capital goods. The emergence of the NICs is illustrative of developments that will influence the direction of export credit negotiation and place new demands on Bank policy.

With varying degrees of enthusiasm, one of the primary goals of the United States over the past few years in the OECD has been to cut off subsidized credits and otherwise limit sales of Western technology to the Soviet Union. U.S. policy on East-West trade has been largely a function of the status of U.S./U.S.S.R relations, whereas most other Western nations take a less political view of trade with the Soviet Union. Markets in the Eastern bloc will continue to be a temptation for capital goods exporters due to the demand for Western technology. U.S. efforts to control technology exports will focus on credits as well as export controls. The emphasis placed on controlling credits has necessitated a compromise on other negotiating objectives. One of the trade-offs in the most recent OECD negotiations was between the increase in interest rates for rich countries combined with the more rigorous reclassification, and maintaining the rate for poor countries with only a small increase for intermediate countries. Continued U.S. emphasis on slowing and ultimately stopping subsidized credit to the Soviet Union is likely to mean less progress in reducing subsidization overall than could have been achieved otherwise.

In addition to these issues, the problems associated with subsidization of capacity and export credits in the U.S. market, discussed in the previous chapter, are also likely to be exacerbated in the future. The effect of a lack of concentrated adjustment programs to reduce excess capacity in basic industries, such as steel in Europe, combined with the continued subsidization of new capacity in the developing countries will lead to a closing of individual markets through protection and increased subsidized competition for U.S. producers. The trade policy problems for the United States will include demands for protection and support for U.S. firms in the basic industries that are fostered by subsidized export credit. There may be little Eximbank can do unilaterally to deter the creation of excess capacity. However, with increasing trade policy problems for all the industrial countries in basic industries such as steel and chemicals, there will be more to be gained from sectoral agreements to limit the subsidization of additional capacity.

The penetration by foreign firms of the U.S. market for capital goods using subsidized credit will continue or even increase until a series of cases signify the firm stand the United States can take to counteract these subsidies. As of this time, several actions are pending with the ITC in the Budd-Bombadier New York subway car case and in small aircraft. A definitive case sending a clear signal to trading partners has not yet emerged. The apparent lack of concern over the disruptive effect of direct subsidies in other major industrial country markets stems from the importance attached to exports by most U.S. competitors. The use of credits in the U.S. market is unlikely to decline until some retaliatory action is taken to influence an important case. Until that time when a clear-cut stand is taken, the pressure of competition with subsidized credit in the U.S. domestic market will bring a series of difficult cases for U.S. trade policy.

Increasing instability in international financial markets, already shaken by major reschedulings, will place added demands on the Bank. A renewed importance in terms of providing access to finance will force some reorientation of Bank policy away from the overriding concern of offsetting foreign subsidies. Such a development may mean a greater risk for Eximbank, and an additional source of claims on limited resources.

All these trends will test the responsiveness of Eximbank policy and its ability to juggle multiple, conflicting objectives and demands. In this environment of increased demands on the Bank the need for careful, deliberate policy planning is paramount. In the past, the Bank has responded to the conflicting demands placed upon it by the formulation of general policy guidelines and a reliance on individual case decisions in an attempt to meet as many of these demands as possible. The result has been an often inconsistent adherence to policies across cases and the succumbing to external pressures. The increasing interrelations between export credits and trade policy issues point to the need for effective and consistent policy planning at the Bank.

Several observers have expressed the view that if economic recovery continues and interest rates remain low, the whole export credits issue will evaporate. In this event there will indeed be an alleviation of demands on the Eximbank as it will be able to charge rates competitive with the Arrangement and yet still earn a profit, as in earlier years. The Bank would also be able to make increased use of guarantees of commercial banks or PEFCO loans, thereby stretching its limited program authority. Opportunities for private-sector participation will be increasingly viable. In the OECD, the United States will be able to press for automatic differentiated means of adjustment of the matrix by playing the recalcitrant role the French have assumed against U.S. efforts to decrease the latitude for subsidization. Even in this situation, however, the longer-term problems of export credit competition and Eximbank policy will remain or reemerge. Export credit problems have never evaporated fully since the concerned export credit and insurance agencies founded the Berne Union in 1934. The need for a more effective means of international control over export credits and the importance of deliberate policy planning resulting in explicit criteria for direct credit support at Eximbank should not be obscured by a temporary easing of economic conditions.

NOTES

1. The limitation on cover is part of the agreement with the Airbus consortium.

2. U.S. Export Import Bank, Policy Analysis Staff, "Follow-Up on Cases Denied Direct Loan Support," November 16, 1981.

Abbreviations

AID	Agency for International Development
AKA	Ausfuhrkredit-Gmbh
BFCE	Banque Francaise du Commerce Exterieur
BIRD	Business and International Review Division
COFACE	Compagnie Francaise d'Assurance pour le Commerce Exterieur
DM	Deutsch mark
DREE	Directions des Relations Economiques Exterieures
DRS	Differentiated Rate System
ECGD	Export Credit Guarantee Department
EEC	European Economic Community
EXIM	Export-Import Bank of Japan
FICA	Federal Insurance Contributions Act
GATT	General Agreement on Tariffs and Trade
GNP	Gross national product
ITA	International Trade Administration
ITC	International Tariff Commission
KfW	Kreditanstalt fur Wiederaubau
LDC	Lesser developed country
LIBOR	London Inter Bank Offered Rate
MAPI	Machinery and Allied Products Institute
MTA	Metropolitan Transit Authority
MTN	Multilateral Trade Negotiations
NAC	National Advisory Council
NICs	Newly industrialized countries
OECD	Organization for Economic Cooperation and Development
OECF	Overseas Economic Corporation Fund
OMB	Office of Management and Budget
PCs	Preliminary commitments
PEFCO	Private Export Funding Corporation
R&D	Research and development
SDR	Special drawing rights
TDP	Trade Development Program
UMM	Uniform Moving Matrix
USTR	U.S. Trade Representative